NEW CAREER OPPORTUNITIES IN HEALTH AND HUMAN SERVICES

NEW CAREER OPPORTUNITIES IN HEALTH AND HUMAN SERVICES

MARGARET DJERF DeRIDDER, M.A.
Assistant Supervisor of
Educational Programs
Woodbridge State School
Woodbridge, New Jersey

ARCO PUBLISHING, INC.
NEW YORK

Published by Arco Publishing, Inc.
215 Park Avenue South, New York, N.Y. 10003

Library of Congress Cataloging in Publication Data

DeRidder, Margaret Djerf.
  New career opportunities in health and human services.

  Includes index.
  1. Social service—Vocational guidance—United
States. 2. Public health—Vocational guidance—United
States. I. Title. [DNLM: 1. Health occupations.
2. Social work. 3. Education, Special. 4. Career
choice. W 21.5 D433n]
HV10.5.D47 1983   361'.0023'73   83-15585
ISBN 0-668-05602-9 (Reference Text)
ISBN 0-668-06103-0 (Paper Edition)

Printed in the United States of America

For my father,
Ero Kullervo Djerf,
who taught me to care.

CONTENTS

ACKNOWLEDGMENTS

There are a number of people whose support and advice have been instrumental in the successful construction of this book. I would particularly like to mention the following people:

Marlene Wiener, for her technical assistance, her photographs, and her endless patience and good humor.

Ellen Lichtenstein, who must surely be one of the most supportive and understanding editors in her profession.

Wilma Pfeffer, Jay Roth, Barbara Lowden, Ted Klein, Joan Herchenroder, Geraldine McCarthy, Joanne Rosenberg, Margaret Armstrong, Anne Arrington, Isabelle DePhillips, and Donald Potenski, who have shared many hours of observation and conversation and helped to shape my understanding of the specifics of their professions.

My sons, Jake and Karl, my mother, and my brother Karl for their constructive criticism and their belief in me.

Dr. John P. Delaney, Superintendent of Woodbridge State School, for his support of this project and his interest in my ideas.

Michael Moroch who never doubted me at all.

NEW CAREER OPPORTUNITIES IN HEALTH AND HUMAN SERVICES

INTRODUCTION

What Do You Want to Be?

You have probably heard that question many times. Walk over to your local playground and ask that question of any group of children. The answers will be fairly predictable. For each child who wants to be an astronaut or an actress, there will be another who looks at you earnestly and says, "I want to help people."

If that sounds like something you might have said, you now may be trying to decide on a career which will meet that goal. Perhaps you are contemplating a career in medicine or in law where your knowledge and expertise will surely help many people. You may also be considering a career in one of the professional areas that are often called *human services*.

If so, then you will find this book helpful. It was designed to give you a clear idea of what people in the "helping professions" do. It also presents a view of the exciting directions that human service careers are taking as they meet new challenges. As you read about these professions, you will be able to decide if you have, or wish to develop, the qualities and skills needed to be successful in one of these rewarding fields.

You will be informed about the training required, as well as the licenses and certifications needed and how to attain them. The range of opportunities available in each profession is presented and, most importantly, salary ranges, job security, and career ladders are detailed.

What Kind of Person Are You?

Helping people is not really the central goal of the human service professional. It is merely a step in the often complex process of helping people learn how to help themselves.

This may sound like a minor distinction, but it is the difference between giving charity and teaching independence. For instance, a gift of money to a needy family or the offer of an arm to help a blind person cross the street are acts that help people through specific emergencies. Just as soon as the money is spent or the blind person reaches the next corner, the need will return. More lasting help is required. Teaching the needy family how to support itself and training the blind person to use a Seeing Eye dog provide more permanent solutions.

Whether you decide to become a social worker, a music therapist, or any of the other professionals described in this book, your job will be aimed at helping people to achieve more control over their own lives. The reward will not be the large sums of money you earn—most salaries in the human services are relatively low—but the intellectual and emotional satisfaction of watching someone grow, gain confidence, and reach out towards independence.

Attributes Needed

Just as you must have musical talent as well as training to become a successful violinist, you must possess certain basic qualities before you consider a career in the helping professions.

Of primary importance is a sincere respect for all human beings. Your work in any of the human service professions will consist of interaction with people. Your major tools will be the skills and abilities you have acquired to assist people as they attempt to solve specific problems or adapt to particular situations. Without a profound regard for the individuality of every person, regardless of who, what, or how impaired he is, you will not be able to establish the rapport that will meet his needs effectively.

Do friends often seek you out when they need to talk? If so, then you probably have a talent for helping them sort out their thoughts. This useful quality is essential to effective communication. There are two kinds of communication skills you must develop.

The first skill is the ability to find the right words to convey exactly what you mean in a way that is helpful to a client rather than discouraging or critical. This is a skill that improves with practice, but you generally need to have a basic openness. An open attitude will make your client feel that you are an honest and trustworthy person.

The second skill is the ability to listen effectively. The people you will be working with may not be able to verbalize their needs very well. You must become skillful at hearing what they are really trying to tell you. You need to be able to read body language and to distinguish between what people say and how they say it. In addition, you must be perceptive enough to tune in on what your client is deliberately *not* saying.

Are you able to sense when friends need more than just a shoulder to lean on? Can you help them feel safe enough to seek the right sort of help? This is the ability known as supportiveness. Being supportive is not just a matter of offering praise or encouragement. You must work at achieving a degree of sensitivity that tells you when people have reached a crisis, need more attention, or are ready to begin assuming responsibility for their own actions.

Objectivity is another essential quality. You must be able to maintain your perspective regardless of your feelings for your clients or about the kind of behavior they exhibit. Therefore, you should have an awareness of your own limitations in order to be sure that your goal of helping your clients deal with their problems does not become a goal of changing the clients to conform to your standards.

Empathy is a very necessary quality for those intending to work with people needing help. Sometimes this quality is confused with sympathy, but there is an important difference. Sympathy is the ability to feel pity or compassion. Empathy, on the other hand, is the ability to see a situation from another person's point of view, regardless of your own feelings. Empathy for the client enables you to provide the sort of experiences that will encourage independent action.

Lastly, dedication is the quality that will help you keep your standards high. Occasionally there are breakthroughs in therapy or treatment that are as exciting as a scientific discovery. Most of the time, however, the human service professional works very hard at a job where day-to-day progress is so slow that it often cannot be seen at all. All of the careers described in this book will test your dedication as well as the other qualities mentioned here.

You must, by now, have an idea whether or not you are the kind of person who will find a career in human services challenging and fulfilling. If you think you are, this book is for you.

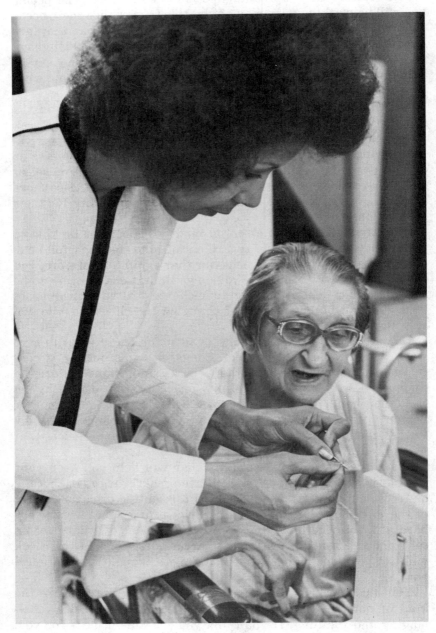

A psychologist works with an older woman in a nursing home. About 30 percent of the elderly have symptoms of depression. (Photo courtesy of the American Psychological Association)

1. WHAT ARE HUMAN SERVICES?

Service to humanity—what a noble phrase! What a gloriously unselfish aim! The words seem to be the absolute antithesis of competition. They evoke images of Albert Schweitzer in the middle of the African jungle and Mother Theresa in a hot and dusty village in India—people working at trying to change human living conditions.

You might not think to include the Rockefeller name on that list of heroes, but there is a gnarled old bus driver in Athens who does. Each day, as he drives his bus full of American tourists into the bare and stony hills of southern Greece, he tells of the poverty and devastation suffered by his family and townspeople after World War II. And he weeps openly with gratitude towards the Rockefellers as he describes how their Foundation rebuilt his town and restored its people to self-sufficiency.

It would be impossible to include here or to define all of the works that could be called human services. Equally difficult would be to make a guess as to when human services first began.

Until the beginning of the 19th century, most human services were provided by the organized church or the medical industry. People who lived on farms and in small villages took care of each other directly—by helping the widow next door get her wheat harvested or by bringing an orphaned child into their own home to raise.

As the rise of industrialism lured people out of rural settings and into cities, almshouses and orphanages were founded. Crowded urban areas not only generated the spread of disease, starvation, and human isolation, but they forced people to depend on a monetary economy. If you had no way of earning money, you had no way to survive.

The gulf between the poor and the rich became much wider at this time. A new class emerged whose fortunes came not from owning land but from manufacturing goods and owning businesses. Women—wealthy, educated, and excluded from the business world because of their sex—turned their attention to the problems of the poor. Their interest lay not merely in giving direct help, but in trying to set up efficient ways to raise money and to achieve more lasting results.

Their attention to the causes and remedies for human suffering helped to force a public acceptance of the obligation to help the less fortunate. Settlement houses and specific services for the helpless began to appear. Retarded children and the mentally ill were recognized as a population in need of care and treatment. This business of providing and maintaining services to improve the lives of the needy led to today's professional social worker.

Today, social work is the central profession in the human services. It is the only career that operates entirely within a human service framework and often provides the staff that coordinates and administrates the other services within an agency. A social worker is often needed to insure that recipients qualify for the services and that their rights are protected. All of the other careers in this book describe specific services.

Human services are those services which help people in need to become as healthy, well-adjusted, and productive as they are capable of being. People seek help from human service professionals or agencies for reasons such as a need for institutional care due to a severe mental or physical disability, assistance for the aged, and help with child adoption proceedings. These services should not be free if the client can afford to pay for them. On the other hand, taxes and contributions are raised to insure that no one is deprived of assistance because of a lack of money.

The philosophy of every organization providing human services is generally based on giving people help, training, therapy, or other assistance in order to maximize their potential to become contributors to society.

Results Rather than Profits

No human service agency functions to make a profit or to create a market for its service. Whenever a program assists a client to overcome a problem, that client no longer needs to use the time of the staff. If all of the services offered by an agency were no longer needed, the agency would no longer need to exist. This does not happen very often. You need not worry that you would be out of a job, because every time a social problem starts to disappear, it seems as if new and more complicated problems are created. For instance, orphan asylums are a relic of the past but the problems of finding and maintaining foster care programs and adoption services have created thousands of private and government jobs.

Most businesses exist to make money. In order to make that money the business may, as in the case of a restaurant, provide a service to people. Most of the time, the better the service and quality of food offered by the restaurant, the more profit it will make.

There is a very good reason why human service agencies and organizations do not function to make a profit. The funds that pay the salaries, buy the equipment, and run the buildings come from taxpayers and contributors. The success of the service provider is judged by the numbers of clients who no longer need to use the service.

Factors Creating Change

Because we are living in a world that is constantly changing, the problems of the people who live in the world keep changing. Human service professionals have to be attuned to all of the shifting directions and trends in order to shape their programs to meet the individual needs of each client.

There are many factors responsible for the changing profile of human service career areas. Some of them have been present for several decades but others are only beginning to indicate the important directions human service professions will take as they move into the 1980's and beyond. Seven trends, in particular, can be shown to have a major impact:

1. The rapid growth and improvements in technology over the past 25 years have changed the picture of American living. The tasks that need to be performed by nurses, social workers, and other human service providers have grown more complicated as well as more specific. The need for technical experts has extended beyond the fields of science and industry, permeating career areas such as law, education, and human services. Professionals in these areas need much more assistance in order to

provide the greater services that are available to people today. The need for specialized training of assistants has led to the new career world of the paraprofessional. These specially trained technicians run the machinery and do the necessary testing in medical services and other scientific fields. They do the vital hours of research and a lot of the legwork in law firms. They operate and repair the equipment used in the increasing number of professions and businesses that utilize computers.

In the area of human services there is also a rapidly growing need for paraprofessionals. The cost of employing a professionally trained person in a task that can be adequately performed by a technician is a major problem for government as well as for private services. Colleges are now beginning to offer a two-year program leading to an A.A.S. degree as a human service worker.

2. The growth of physical, psychological, and occupational therapies as a vital part of treating problems and restoring abilities has led to career areas where highly specialized training is mandatory. These fields are growing rapidly and employing professionals, paraprofessionals, and specialists in hospitals, schools, institutions, and agencies.

3. The change in public sentiment and philosophy from the expansionism of the welfare programs throughout the 1950's and 1960's to the conservatism of the 1980's has had a marked effect on the human services. The decentralization of programs is causing changes in job availability. The need for more effective and creative use of available funds is placing greater demands on individuals who are employed in all human service areas.

4. Another factor somewhat related to the above is the trend toward deinstitutionalization. This is having a major impact on traditional job areas in mental hospitals and institutions for the retarded. While some jobs are disappearing and services are being curtailed as these large facilities are being depopulated, there is a growing need for services to group and foster home clients and to assist communities to move towards greater involvement with and acceptance of these clients.

The philosophy of normalization holds that the more normally people are treated, the more normal they will

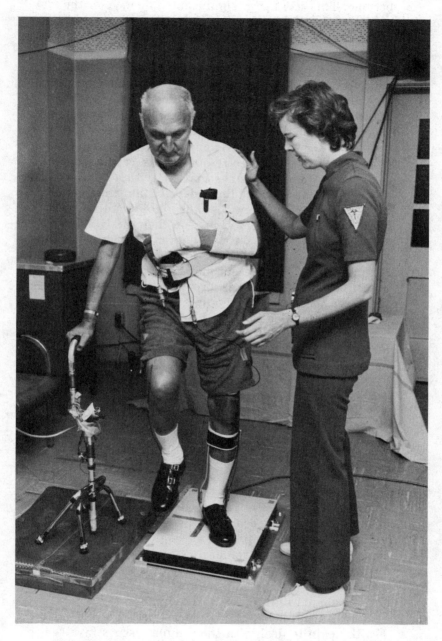

Force plate and force care measurements are taken by physical therapist to determine body weight on a cane. (Photo courtesy of the American Physical Therapy Association)

become. This has had a significant influence on the way public and private services have moved towards decentralization. All institutions, whether they be prisons, mental hospitals, residential schools for the retarded, nursing homes, etc., tend to create a rigidly structured, artificial, and often dehumanizing world for the people who live in them. Clients are sometimes fed, dressed, bathed, programmed, and housed according to the functional needs of the institution and the working shifts of the staff. Very little provision used to be made for the changing needs and desires of clients concerning diet, clothing preferences, or social activities. The people living in these surroundings develop an "institutionalized" outlook. They may lose their ability to make even simple choices. The emptiness of their daily lives may cause them to take on peculiar mannerisms and behaviors which make them appear "different" from normal people. The present movement to normalize these institutionalized people is breaking down the barriers that keep these groups of people from being accepted by society as individuals of worth and dignity.

Moving people out of large, isolated residential placements and into small, homelike living situations located in residential neighborhoods is one of the major ways that the living situations of the handicapped can become normalized. Providing them with real and meaningful occupation and socialization within the community setting is another. This movement is creating a need for greater and richer community services in the areas of occupational and recreational therapy, as well as a need for more community social workers, visiting nurses, homemakers, and psychological counselors.

Institutions themselves are also changing to be more responsive to the needs and development of the individual. This is accomplished through enriched programming services and a refocusing of the purposes of the institution from the segregation of a group of people from society to that of providing greater opportunities for the clients to interact in the community.

Even as the fields of mental retardation and mental health begin to deal with the complex issues involved in deinstitutionalization, there appears to be a faint trend towards reversing some of the decentralized services which have been altering the fields of correction and services to delinquent children. The public is taking a harder look at people who break the law and is inclined to regard some of the rehabilitative programs of the 1960's and 1970's as too lenient. Correctional institutions are becoming overcrowded, young offenders are being tried in court as adults more frequently, and discipline is tightening in schools across the country.

It is difficult to predict all of the ways that social workers, therapists, psychologists, and other professionals will have to adapt their services as the needs and attitudes of society continue to change.

5. Geriatric nursing and counseling—care and assistance for the aged—is one of the fastest growing areas in the field of human services and has led to new career possibilities. Hospice programs, although not limited to any specific age group, provide specialized assistance in helping terminally ill people and their families to face and get through this shattering life experience. These programs are now becoming more available to people in all parts of the country.

6. Recent legislation such as the Education for All Handicapped Children Act of 1975 (Public Law 94-142), as well as Title III of the Older Americans Act, has opened up all sorts of educational, social, and employment areas for the disabled, handicapped, aged, and other populations needing special services. It is also responsible for creating career areas in those professions which administrate the programs and provide the services. For example, all children, regardless of their handicapping condition, are now required by law to have regular education programs developed for them on an individualized basis after classification and evaluation by a proper child study team. Individualized Education Plans (I.E.P.) are provided by special education teachers and other specialized professionals such as speech therapists, occupational and physical therapists, and psychologists. Many children who used to be kept at home are now receiving a broad range of educational services in public and private schools. Professionals are needed to provide services for them.

7. Lastly, all of our modern social problems—from unemployment and drug addiction to runaway children and
broken homes—are conditions that influence the varieties
of human services we have as well as the directions they
will take in the future. Television, in addition to improved social services, has created a more enlightened
and demanding service population. News programs and
informative educational channels provide the public with
knowledge about social problems and about the programs
available to combat them. Government organizations and
programs such as VISTA, CETA, the Head Start program, and the food stamp program reach many needy
people by publicizing their rights to treatment, assistance, and education.

Finding answers to today's problems, coordinating and
consolidating necessary services, and anticipating emerging needs are the challenging areas you will deal with
if you decide on a career in human services.

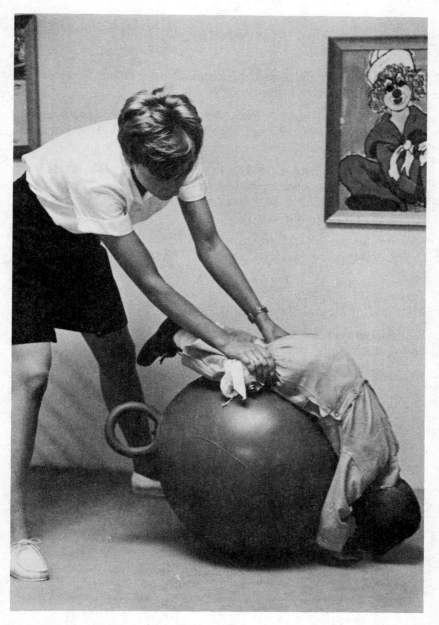

A child learns arm coordination by being suspended over a beach ball. This is one method of employing motor reflexes to initiate movement in children who are brain-damaged or lacking in coordination. (Photo courtesy of the American Physical Therapy Association)

References

Holmes, M., and Holmes, D. *Handbook of Human Services for Older Persons*. Human Sciences Press, 1979.

Magreb, P., and Elder, J. *Planning for Services to Handicapped Persons: Community, Education, Health*. Paul H. Brookes Publishing Co., Inc., 1979.

President's Committee on Mental Retardation. *MR 78 Mental Retardation: The Leading Edge. Service Programs That Work*. U.S. Department of Health, Education, and Welfare, U.S. Government Printing Office, 1978.

Scheerenberger, R.C. *Managing Residential Facilities for the Developmentally Disabled*. Charles C. Thomas, 1975.

Wolfensberger, W. *A Look into the Future for Systems of Human Services With Special Reference to Mental Retardation*. National Institute on Mental Retardation, Canada, 1973.

Wolfensberger, W. *The Principle of Normalization in Human Services*. National Institute on Mental Retardation, Canada, 1972.

2. THE CLASSIC HUMAN SERVICE PROFESSIONS

Social Work, Clinical Psychology, Special Education, Nursing, and Nutrition

Most human service jobs are located within government agencies and departments. If you work in a state or federal hospital, institution, or agency, regardless of your profession, your salary will be paid by the government and will come directly from taxes.

Human service careers in the private sector may be found in a very complex and wide-ranging group of private agencies which employ teachers, therapists, psychologists, social workers, nutritionists, and others. Salaries in these agencies are generally paid with money directly funded by the government, secured through grants, or raised by the agency or its auxiliaries as donations. You may be a full-time or a part-time employee. Your service may be provided under an hourly contract or you may be a permanent employee.

Human service jobs are found in all parts of the country. Most of them, however, are in or near cities because more services are needed in urban areas. Every state offers both public and private services.

In this chapter you will read about ten professional areas in the human services. Some of these careers have been around for many years but are taking new directions to meet the social needs of today. Others are very new and becoming more important as technological knowledge increases.

Included for each career is a description of the kinds of activities that characterize the job, the education and training needed for licensing or certification, and different directions you can take once you enter the field.

Since jobs in this area are greatly influenced by the economic condition of the country and political attitudes of the voting citizens, some of the problems of the field are discussed honestly and with an eye to the competition you will face.

Especially stressed will be the new areas of technology within established professions, where the jobs are at the present time, and how to go about finding one. Salaries in the field will be included as far as is possible. Variations in salary depend on the geographic location of the job and whether or not it is in the private or public sector.

Also, in order to help you picture yourself as one of the professionals mentioned in the book, some real life experiences of human service workers are included.

Social Work

A Case in Point

On this clear, sunny spring morning the cherry blossoms give the grounds of the institution a festive air in keeping with your high hopes for the events taking place on this day. Many of the young retarded clients living in the 15 one-story brick cottages are walking or playing with staff members. Everyone seems to be enjoying the chance to be outside after the long, cold winter.

Parking the state car carefully in front of Cottage 12, you smile sociably at two foster grandmothers in bright blue smocks who are pushing a pair of young girls in wheelchairs towards a sunlit bench. You walk up the short path to the front door of the cottage where the head cottage training supervisor is waiting for you.

"I'm here," you call cheerfully. "Is John ready to leave for the group home?"

"He sure is," answers Mrs. Williams. "He's been sitting with his suitcase in his lap ever since breakfast was over. He's so excited about leaving they tell me he hardly slept a wink. I sure hope it works out for him."

A quick phone call to John's group leader notifies the staff in the back of the cottage that John is leaving. All of a sudden the small foyer is growing crowded with people. The nurse is there with John's medication and allergy information. The tearful group leader arrives carrying a winter jacket and a large candy bar. John trudges in carrying a brand-new plaid suitcase as if it were made of glass. Two other staff members show up, as well as several of John's friends who want to wave him off.

It is a bittersweet moment for all of the people who have been taking care of John since he came to the institution 15 years ago.

John, however, appears to be taking the moment with his usual happy approach to life. His short brown hair has been neatly combed, and his brown suit and yellow shirt were bought specially for this occasion. He kisses everyone good-bye, giving an emotional hug to his group leader and carefully pocketing the candy bar in exchange. As John heads out of the door to the car, Mrs. Williams hands you another sheaf of papers to add to John's file.

As you start the car, you glance over at this small, sturdy young man with Down's Syndrome who appears much younger than his 23 years. He is grinning broadly at everyone as they stand at the door waving at him. He is so eager to be off that he is jumping up and down in his seat. You hope with all your heart that John will adjust quickly and not miss his companions and the routine of institutional living too much.

John has no idea how hard you have been working to find this home for him. He is one of 17 young men from that cottage for whom you have been trying to find community placements. Your pleasure over this trip is well-earned. Good group homes are still not very easy to find although their numbers are increasing all the time. Retarded people, like John, who have lived most of their lives in institutions often have a harder time being accepted in, as well as adjusting to, group home situations than retarded people who have lived at home with their families. This is because many institutionalized people do not have much opportunity to learn to be independent and to assume responsibility.

Although John has been cared for by a loving and dedicated staff of people, and despite the fact that his elderly, widowed mother visits him frequently and brings him home for holidays, he has become used to moving and living as part of a group. Also, his small size and severe retardation have made it easy for people to expect childish behavior from him. John has never learned to separate his clothes or belongings from those of the seven other young men in his group. He has never poured himself a glass of milk or changed the dial on the day-room television set because these things are always done for him. He does not even know how to turn off a water tap because all of the faucets in the cottage turn off automatically.

John will now begin a new life in a large, ordinary house on a typical street in an average American community. He has been preparing for this adventure by learning a hierarchy of self-help and vocational skills that most people master well before they reach school age. His handicaps have made it hard for him to learn. But the biggest handicap of all has been the years of practice John has missed to develop independent living skills.

As you reflect on the problems ahead for John, you also review the progress you have made. It took many phone calls to state and private agencies to locate a group home in an area of the state convenient enough for John's mother to visit frequently.

It also took a great deal of skill and understanding on your part to help John's mother overcome her fears about taking him away from the safety of the institution where she felt he would be watched over even when she was gone.

Since the group home is located in the middle of town, John will be learning to cross streets, shop for his own toiletries, attend a neighborhood church, and even walk to a nearby sheltered workshop where he will put his vocational training to use and earn wages commensurate with his ability and speed.

You have worked with the institutional staff as well as the staff in the group home to make the transition period as smooth as possible. John's individual needs have been thoroughly discussed, the vocational placement has been visited, and John and his mother have been to visit the young men who live in the home and to meet the staff who will now be working with John.

As the social worker assigned to John's cottage, you have a caseload that ranges from 35 to 50 young men, depending on whether or not the cottage is overcrowded. It is your responsibility to maintain close contact with John's mother and the other parents or relatives of the clients in the cottage. You are also responsible for insuring that your clients' money is properly taken care of and that their habilitation needs are met according to the regulations and policies of the state. You also must see that community placements allow each client the opportunity to develop to as high a potential as possible and in the least restrictive setting he can manage.

It is this last goal you are attempting to meet as you drive John to his new home. Once he has passed a six-week trial period you will cease to be John's caseworker, and a different social worker will be responsible for insuring that John's needs are met and that his human rights are not violated.

The state car passes through the gates of the institution and out into the busy morning traffic. In the back seat, the nurse smooths her skirt and settles down for a long ride. She has asked to come along in order to give a last minute briefing to the people who will help John learn to take his own medication. John's eyes are resolutely looking forward. This day, you decide, is one of the days when it all comes together. This is why you chose to be a social worker.

What Do Social Workers Do?

The role of the social worker in the human services is of paramount importance. Social workers plan, administer, and facilitate services to needy people. Their work may be with individuals, families, groups, or communities. They may also work to improve community services and resources. They arrange for medical, financial, or rehabilitative assistance. They refer clients for services such as counseling or health care. They assist individuals and their families in handling problems related to mental illness, physical disability, recovery, death, and unemployment.

Social workers may work directly with people on a one-to-one or a family basis. This is generally called casework and consists of interviewing individuals or families to identify and help solve problems. Caseworkers must be adept at locating and securing the appropriate services or assistance.

Social workers also work with groups of people who have similar problems or interests such as diabetics or people in preventive programs. They plan and run programs and activities for people of all ages such as groups in nursing homes, hospitals, or teenage organizations.

You may also perform social work on the behalf of people. You may be coordinating the work of local civic and community groups in order to solve social problems. You may be planning or administrating health, welfare, and other major services to communities, states, and federal government programs.

Most social workers perform some direct services and some indirect services. They all collaborate with a variety of health and educational professionals in order to plan and provide the best possible care. Whether a social worker is employed by the federal government, state government, county, community, school, or private organization, he must not only be able to work with all kinds of people but must have the patience and emotional stability to deal with rules, regulations, and mountains of red tape.

Where Do You Find Jobs?

Social workers are employed by private and public welfare agencies, hospitals and clinics, institutions, community centers, schools and colleges, public health departments and programs, long and short term care facilities, and in private practice.

In private agencies and hospitals you will probably be required to do a combination of direct and administrative services. You

Finding appropriate work or home placements for clients can be the most demanding part of the social worker's job. (Photo by Marlene Wiener)

may also run groups or collaborate with other community services.

When you are employed under the jurisdiction of a state or other governmental authority, your position may involve field and office work, investigations, collection and analysis of data, and documentation of social facts. You may elect to work in a specific service area such as a department of mental health or housing, or with a specific program such as drug abuse or battered children.

Most social work jobs are found in urban areas but there are public and private service agencies throughout the United States.

Education

In order to become a professional social worker, you must have a minimum of a bachelor's degree in social work (B.S.W.). The B.S.W. program will provide coursework in the areas of social work practice, social welfare and service, human behavior, environmental problems of society, social research, and supervised field experience. A B.S.W. program will prepare you for an entry-level position as a caseworker or group worker. You may also qualify for an entry-level job if you have a degree in the liberal arts or humanities such as sociology or psychology.

A master's degree in social work (M.S.W.) is preferred or required for many positions and necessary to advance to higher-level supervisory or administrative positions. Two years of specialized study and supervised field instruction are required to earn an M.S.W. A number of graduate schools offer health concentrations. Applicants to graduate programs in social work may face stiff competition.

A graduate degree plus experience are necessary for supervisory and top administrative positions. Training in social science research methods is essential for research positions.

If you plan to teach, direct a program, or run an agency, a Ph.D. is usually required.

In government agencies, most applicants for employment must pass a written examination except for some high-level positions. Twenty states require licensing or registration.

The National Association of Social Workers grants certification and the title A.C.S.W. (Academy of Certified Social Workers) to members who have a master's degree, at least two years of post-master's experience, and who have passed the A.C.S.W. examination. Efforts are now being made to devise specialized examinations because of the increasing trend towards specialization at higher levels of practice.

Employment Outlook

Job opportunities for social workers should continue to be good through the mid-1980's. The competition for jobs will be keen and the economic situation as well as deinstitutionalization will be responsible for a shift in the geographic location of available jobs. The expansion of services in the community and in the public schools should contribute to new employment. Increased public awareness and demand for services to the aged, the handicapped, and the unemployed should also result in new positions for social workers. Other areas where the need for social workers is increasing can be found in services for counseling of drug addicts, rape victims, and other groups of troubled people.

Salaries for social workers at all levels vary greatly depending on the type of agency and the geographic location. Average earnings for social workers with a bachelor's degree may range from $10,000 to $14,000. For psychiatric social workers and casework supervisors, which require a master's degree, starting salaries range from $12,000 to about $15,000. Experienced social workers average about $20,000 and up.

Salaries in federal and state government positions are usually higher than those of social workers who work for private agencies.

The majority of social workers have a five-day, 35-hour to 40-hour week. In private agencies, there may be part-time jobs, or the nature of duties may require evening or weekend work. Nearly all of the agencies provide paid vacation, sick leave, retirement plans, and hospitalization programs.

Additional Information

For additional information about career opportunities in the field of social work contact:

National Association of Social Workers
1425 H Street, NW
Washington, D.C. 20005

Council on Social Work Education
345 East 46th Street
New York, NY 10017

References

Bartlett, H. *The Common Base of Social Work Practice*. National Association of Social Workers, 1970.

Dickerson, M. *Social Work Practice With the Mentally Retarded*. The Free Press, 1981.

Holmes, M., and Holmes, D. *Handbook of Human Services for Older Persons*. Human Sciences Press, 1979.

Morales, A., and Sheafor, B. *Social Work, A Profession of Many Faces*. Allyn and Bacon, Inc., 1977.

Morris, R. "The Place of Social Work in Human Services" in *Social Work*. Vol. 19, September 1974.

Wolfensberger, W. *The Principle of Normalization in Human Services*. National Institute on Mental Retardation, Canada, 1972.

Clinical Psychology

One of the Group

Sitting comfortably in the old leather chair, you study the members of the therapy group as they arrive. Although you do not look as if you are working, your eyes and ears have been trained to notice minute details in behavior. The way a person walks into a room, the hesitancies in speech, or the outfit someone has chosen to wear may all signal a change or a setback in that person's progress in therapy. It is your job to file these observations in your mind, compare them with your knowledge about the client and, perhaps, bring them to light later on as the evening session progresses.

Brenda is wearing make-up and has a new hairstyle. This is a good sign, you note to yourself. She appears to be livelier and more outgoing than usual as she indignantly tells Amy about an unpleasant encounter she had during the day.

Amy, on the other hand, seems to be trying to melt into the background as she listens. She will nod agreement with Brenda's assessment of the situation regardless of what she is thinking. She always seems terrified of what might happen if she were to oppose any point of view, or to suggest one of her own. Amy is wearing jeans and a brown sweater that is as nondescript as everything about her. You wonder to yourself what she would look like in a bright red dress but cannot even picture it in your mind.

As the two women stand in the center of the room, Martin strides angrily through the door. He sits down abruptly in a chair near you and stares impatiently at the ceiling. As his feet tap a staccato rhythm on the floor and his fingers twitch at his sides, he seems about to explode.

Elizabeth has followed Martin into the room. A large, middle-aged woman in sensible shoes, she sits down heavily on the couch. Looking around the room, she smiles a greeting at you and says hello to Brenda and Amy. She does not venture a word to Martin.

As Brenda settles down on the couch near Elizabeth, Amy sits quietly on the floor near the two women. Knees drawn up to her chin, arms wound tightly around them, she looks very small and afraid.

Everyone glances at the door as Jeff comes in. This is his first evening here and he seems very reluctant to meet anyone. He sits close to the door, carefully averting his eyes from you.

It is eight o'clock. Martha is not here yet but you decide not to wait for her. She is often late and frequently tries to call attention to herself with spectacular entrances. You remind yourself to speak to her at the end of the evening about coming for private therapy. She does not seem to be getting anywhere in a group situation and her behavior is not helpful to the cohesiveness of the others.

"Shall we start?" you inquire.

For a minute or two the room is quiet. Tension seems to be building. The only sounds are the muffled street noises outside.

Then Martin begins: "I'm not coming here any longer," he states belligerently. "I'm not getting anywhere and I could use the time I'm wasting to do lots of other things."

"What other things?" counters Brenda.

The atmosphere in the room becomes charged with emotion as the members of the group begin to warm up. This is not the first time Martin has begun a session this way and some of the members sense his need to have them urge him to continue. No one has any idea of the direction the evening will take but most of them are hoping that, somehow, it will be a special session for them.

All of the members except Jeff have been coming once a week for quite some time, and although none of them know each other outside of the group, they are used to interacting. The support of the members of the group helps each person to disclose the aspects of himself or his life that he wishes to change or to face. Your expertise is necessary to guide the individual members towards the directions most helpful to themselves and to insure that the group remains a positive experience for all.

There are many benefits of this type of therapy, not the least of which is its relative affordability to clients. It also enables you to use the same time for a number of people.

Tonight you are planning to encourage Jeff to talk a little about himself. In the private session that you had with him several days ago, he mentioned his reluctance to meet people and his fears about what others thought of him. Your experience with the warmth and supportiveness that characterize most group therapy situations led you to suggest that he come tonight. The two of you then discussed some of the specific ways he could use the group to deal with his fears. You also reassured him that he would retain complete control over how much or how little he chose to participate.

This therapy group is only one segment of your career as a clinical psychologist. You are a valued member of the faculty at a nearby college and also are affiliated with the county mental health organization. Staff psychologists there refer young adults and some adolescents to you for direct therapy.

Although your schedule is very demanding and the long years of training were expensive and difficult, your work as a clinical psychologist is intellectually rewarding and financially comfortable.

What Do Psychologists Do?

Psychologists study the individual and group behaviors of humans and animals in order to understand, explain, and predict their actions. Regardless of the area in which they specialize, all psychologists use scientific methods to discover the causes of behavior. The information they study is gathered through interviews, tests, controlled experiments, statistical studies, and direct observation.

Psychologists may specialize in a variety of areas. There are exciting career opportunities in experimental, industrial, and social psychology. The specialty which is a vital part of human services, however, is that of the clinical psychologist. Related specialties are those of the school psychologist and the counseling psychologist.

Clinical psychology is concerned with the diagnosis and treatment of mental and emotional problems. Clinical psychologists are trained to conduct research and may also teach, consult, and supervise mental health programs. Most clinical psychologists work in psychiatric hospitals, outpatient clinics, university counseling centers, rehabilitation centers, and other health facilities. Others work for federal, state, and local government agencies, institutions, and in private practice.

Although there is a lot of competition for good positions, employment in this field is expected to continue to grow throughout the 1980's, especially for those holding doctoral degrees.

Range of Activities

Testing

A psychologist is needed whenever important decisions have to be made concerning a person's ability. Psychologists are employed to test whether a child is retarded, whether a suspect knows right from wrong, or whether a college student has an aptitude for marine biology.

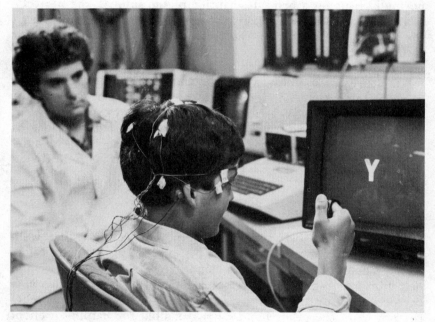

To diagnose and correct reading problems, this psychologist works with a hyperactive child at a Children's Hospital. In this test, the child's ability to identify letters of the alphabet is being monitored by the EEG's and by his thumb-press response. (Photo courtesy of the American Psychological Association)

Clinicians administer batteries of tests that may include intelligence tests, projective tests which reveal important information about attitudes, feelings, and other aspects of personality development, and measures of specific motor coordination. These tests help to determine whether a person is showing signs of brain damage as in the case of motor or perceptual impairment. Aptitude and interest tests may also be included.

These tests are generally administered on an individual basis in order to provide information for a specific purpose. When the battery is completed, the psychologist must score the tests, interpret the data, and write a report of the findings. This report normally includes a brief description of the subject, the subject's attitude toward the examiner, the subject's behavior throughout the testing, the results of the tests, and a recommendation for future treatment.

School psychologists often do this kind of testing. They may work closely with a child's teacher and the school social worker in order to develop individualized programs for slow learners or troubled children. A school psychologist, however, does not normally engage in formal psychotherapy. For legal reasons as well as because of their large caseloads, the school psychologist will refer a child for treatment whenever therapy is indicated.

Psychotherapy and Counseling

The distinction between therapy and counseling is not well-defined. It often depends upon the person making the distinction. In most definitions, however, a counselor works with a person to help him make important decisions concerning his life such as a career choice or whether or not to seek a divorce. A psychotherapist, on the other hand, is responsible for helping a client to recognize and change unacceptable or self-defeating behaviors.

Education

A bachelor's degree with a major in psychology is only the beginning for someone who is serious about a career as a clinical psychologist. In addition, the student should include coursework in statistics, computer science, and biology. Among undergraduate psychology courses, he must include developmental, abnormal, and experimental psychology. Graduate schools will

The school psychologist's expertise in assessment aids in correct academic placement for the child. (Photo by Marlene Wiener)

be particularly interested in your grades in experimental psychology as an indication of aptitude for research.

With a B.A. degree you will be qualified for limited jobs as a research or administrative assistant in mental health centers, vocational rehabilitation centers, and correctional facilities. If you complete state certification requirements, you may be able to teach at the secondary school level.

In order to be admitted to a graduate program, you must have grades of B or better, good recommendations, and satisfactory scores on the Graduate Record Examination and the Miller Analogies Test. Volunteer experience or work in clinical settings will also be helpful.

Once you have obtained a master's degree, you are qualified to work under the supervision of a psychologist, collect and analyze data, and administer and interpret certain tests. You may also qualify for some counseling positions such as school psychologist.

Ph.D. programs are accredited by the American Psychological Association. In order to earn a Ph.D. in psychology, you must complete three to five years of additional graduate work. Clinical and counseling psychologists must also have another year or more of internship or other supervised experience. The American Psychological Association evaluates facilities and approves internships.

A dissertation based on original research that will contribute to psychological knowledge is required for a Ph.D. If a Psy.D. (Doctor of Psychology) is granted, it is based on practice and examinations rather than a dissertation.

The American Board of Professional Psychology awards diplomas in clinical counseling and school psychology. State certification and licenses vary but generally require a Ph.D. or Psy.D., two years of professional experience, and a written exam.

Certification laws do not regulate the practice of psychotherapy. There are still many states where there are hardly any restrictions on who can offer services as a psychotherapist, a counselor, or a hypnotist.

Employment Outlook

The variation in income for psychologists is so great that it is impossible to predict average salaries. With a master's degree, starting salaries are about $14,000 per year. Beginning salaries for a Ph.D. range from $17,000 to $22,000 at clinics and hospitals.

An average salary for an experienced psychologist with a doctoral degree is about $23,000 in an educational institution, $30,000 in state and local government agencies, and $25,000 and up in hospitals, clinics, and nonprofit organizations. Average fees for private practice are $35.00 to $75.00 per hour depending on the type of counseling or therapy and the geographic location.

Additional Information

For additional information about career opportunities in clinical psychology contact:

American Psychological Association
1200 17th Street, NW
Washington, DC 20036

National Association of School Psychologists
1511 K Street, NW
Washington, DC 20005

American Board of Professional Psychology
2025 Eye Street, NW, Suite 405
Washington, DC 20006

References

Balthazar, E., and Stevens, H. *The Emotionally Disturbed, Mentally Retarded: A Historical and Contemporary Perspective.* Prentice-Hall, Inc., 1975.

Greenspan, S., and Pollock, G. (Eds.). *The Course of Life; Psychoanalytic Contributions Towards Understanding Personality Development.* U.S. Department of Health and Human Services, 1981.

Johnson, D.W. *Reaching Out; Interpersonal Effectiveness and Self-Actualization.* Prentice-Hall, Inc., 1972.

Long, J., Morse, W., and Newman, R. *Conflict in the Classroom: The Education of Emotionally Disturbed Children.* 3rd ed., Wadsworth Publishing Co., Inc., 1976.

Pietrofesa, J., Leonard, G., and Van Hoose, W. *The Authentic Counselor.* Rand McNally Co., 1971.

Pruyser, P. *The Psychological Examination; A Guide for Clinicians.* International Universities Press, Inc., 1979.

Rogers, C. *On Encounter Groups.* Perennial Library, Harper and Row Publishers, Inc., 1970.

Schmolling, P., Burger, W., and Youkeles, M. *Helping People: A Guide to Careers in Mental Health.* Prentice-Hall, Inc., 1981.

Special Education

A Branch Off the Mainstream

As you open the door of your classroom at 8:30 a.m., the morning sunlight outlines the small collection of stunted plants on the windowsill. Actually, they are marigolds, started two months ago from seeds planted in milk cartons by the six multiply handicapped children in your class. They are supposed to be in bloom by Mother's Day but, so far, they have had a very hard life. You smile to yourself as you reflect on how many times an angry, upset child has thrown his or someone else's plant across the room and then, anger spent, has hopefully retrieved the battered milk carton, scooped the dirt back around the straggly roots, and placed the plant back on the windowsill with the others. Overwatered during the week and dried out during the weekends and holidays, the plants survive almost miraculously.

Just like the children in your class, you think, coming each morning to this special school where, for five hours a day, they learn how to relax the guard they keep over themselves.

Six children may not seem like much of a problem to teach, but your class, like all of the others in the school, consists of six children who display six different disabilities, six different kinds of behavior, and need six individualized learning programs.

Sitting down at your desk, you open your plan book and check your program. This is one of the most important parts of your day. For half an hour or so each morning you review each child's daily progress against his Individual Education Plan (I.E.P.) and make any necessary adjustments to your schedule.

You notice that Billy is nearly finished with his book about Houdini. Remembering how afraid Billy was to read aloud at the beginning of the school year, you feel very pleased that yesterday he demanded that you listen to the story he had written. You make a note in your plan book to drive to the library with him on his "special hour" so that he can select a new book.

In the margin of the plan book, you have indicated that a child study team member from Sally's school district will be visiting this afternoon to see if she will be ready to return to public school in September. You have high hopes for Sally this time as her behavior has improved consistently and she has begun to talk about when she is "back in a *real* school again."

Sally never has seemed to have any of the neurological or

perceptual problems exhibited by so many of the children in the school. She is not psychotic, but she certainly has been disturbed. When she first arrived in your class two years ago she averaged four or five angry, acting-out episodes every day, and you often arrived home after school feeling totally exhausted.

Sally's problems started shortly after her mother died and her father took her across town to live with his elderly parents. All of the abrupt changes in her life seemed to be too much for Sally. She began exhibiting many aggressive behaviors, especially at her new school. When she threw a chair at her teacher and narrowly missed hurting a classmate, she was referred to the school psychologist who recommended placement in a special education program where her emotional problems could be treated.

Sally's school district was small and had no special class that suited her, so a placement was found in the private day school where you teach. A therapy program was begun with the clinical psychologist on your staff and Sally's father and grandparents were encouraged to participate.

You will miss her straightforward nature and her quick wit, but you feel very glad that she has come so far and are certain that she will make it back to public school this fall.

Andrew may be going back to his school also. He really isn't able to compete in an ordinary third grade but his district will be opening up a class for neurologically impaired children and he will be able to participate in many of the regular school activities.

Jill and Philip were new to your class this year and are only beginning to feel at home with you. Jill is a slight, elfin child with a severe language disability, and Philip has a number of neurological problems as well as a host of fears and phobias.

Mark is one of the most difficult children you have ever taught. A handsome, blond boy, 12 years old, his behavior is mercurial. One minute he is alert, interested, and working hard on his lessons; the next minute he is attacking one of his classmates for no apparent reason. His psychotic episodes seem to be occurring more frequently and with greater intensity. You reluctantly decide that a case conference must be called. Perhaps a change in program or therapy is indicated. The psychiatrist who had worked with Mark before he came to your class may have some advice. You make a mental note to have her contacted prior to the conference.

The slam of a door at the end of the hall and the sound of running feet warn you that the buses are beginning to arrive. You also hear the calm voice of your assistant as she comforts Philip, who has been teased by Mark.

As you rise to go to the doorway, Billy bustles in with a shoebox under his arm. "Hey!" he shouts, "wait 'til you see my snake! His name is Fred." You smile weakly. It is only 9 a.m.

The Teacher of the Handicapped

Exciting changes are taking place in the field of special education which hold promise for the quality of education provided to children with mental, physical, and emotional handicaps. The knowledge and experience gleaned from the past 20 years of state and federally mandated special education services have been making an impact in many directions.

Colleges and universities are beginning to recognize the need for greater depth in specialization. Special education certification programs are reflecting this awareness by narrowing the field covered by the certificate.

Thirty-five years ago, a teacher with an elementary school certificate was expected to be able to teach any child under high school age whose disabilities did not require him to stay at home or to be institutionalized. As early as 1900 there were some classes and schools for the retarded, but these were mostly in large urban areas. Very few of the teachers working with the retarded received any special training other than an additional course or two and whatever direct experience they could find.

The inclusion of Trainable Mentally Retarded (T.M.R.) programs in public schools began at the end of the 1940's, but it took another ten years before federal legislation provided money for additional programs to teach the handicapped and to train leadership personnel in the education of the retarded. By the middle of the 1960's, most colleges and universities offering degree programs towards educational certificates had special education departments.

Whom Do You Teach?

The major focus of the first special education programs was on the training of the retarded, yet many other exceptionalities were being identified as well. The decade of the 1970's witnessed a tremendous growth in research, program design, legislation, and often opposing philosophies for the treatment and education of the handicapped.

Working with special children is always challenging and often just plain fun. (Photo by Marlene Wiener, courtesy of Woodbridge State School)

At present, the population of handicapped children includes those who are mentally retarded, blind or visually handicapped, speech impaired, deaf or hard-of-hearing, emotionally disturbed, orthopedically handicapped, health impaired, and children with developmental or specific learning disabilities.

What Will You Be Teaching?

As a teacher of the handicapped you will be expected to plan and implement individualized learning programs for each student in your class. You will be providing academic instruction, if possible, as well as individual and group experiences. You must be familiar with special and adaptive equipment, as needed, and be committed to helping each child develop to his highest potential. You will have to be concerned with the social development and health of your students and will be required to work to resolve behavior, personality, and self-help problems. Also, you must always be familiar with the etiology and symptoms of each disability so as to be alert to conditions that need attention.

If you are teaching in a self-contained classroom, you will ordinarily have one or more assistants who work under your direct supervision. If you work as part of a team teaching system or as a resource room teacher, you will also be working very closely with other teachers.

You will be expected to consult with parents, specialists, and your immediate supervisor as well as with the child study team or other evaluative teams responsible for programs. You will attend meetings and conferences, keep detailed attendance and progress records, and may be asked to supervise playground and lunchroom activities. Because special classes are small and programs tend to be experiential, you will probably spend much more time planning field trips than other teachers.

As a teacher of the handicapped you are presumed to be qualified and may be required to teach any of the previously mentioned disabilities. It is not at all unusual to have a class composed of children with different handicaps who display a range of behaviors, academic abilities, and program needs.

The Education for All Handicapped Children Act of 1975 mandates that every child in your program must have an Individualized Education Plan (I.E.P.). In addition, the requirements of the Act specify that handicapped children receive their special program in the least restrictive environment. This is breaking down the historically segregated "special class" in favor of main-streaming the child into as much of the regular public school program as he can handle.

Where Are the Jobs?

Mainstreaming, decentralization, better prenatal care, a smaller school population, and the currently depressed economy are having a dramatic negative effect on the job market for teachers. Today, a new teacher with certification in special education as well as early childhood education has the best chance of finding employment. There is a need for skilled professionals in the area of early childhood education for the handicapped child. There is also a shortage of minority and bilingual special educators.

The more severely handicapped children continue to be found in traditional self-contained classes where they appear to function best. There are many private day and residential schools for this population. Jobs are frequently advertised, but the competition is stiff and the salaries are not as high as those in local public school systems or state-run day schools.

State institutions for the retarded, state mental hospitals, and correctional institutions may employ special education teachers although job opportunities are becoming scarce because of the trend towards educating in the least restrictive environment.

It is still possible for a teacher of the handicapped to move from teaching one disability to another, but this is becoming more difficult as the body of knowledge needed to be an effective teacher of each specialty area increases. Some states already require certification in a particular specialty.

Educating the Educator

In order to teach classified children you must have at least a bachelor's degree and certification that conforms to state laws for teaching the handicapped. Many colleges and universities are beginning to offer programs that give additional training and supervised experience in specialized areas such as the severely and profoundly retarded, the deaf, and the blind. These programs are generally above the bachelor's level and may lead to a master's degree with emphasis in one specialty area.

If you are already teaching, part or all of your additional training may be paid for by your school system, or you may receive salary increments for credits above certification.

Because of the competition for jobs, most school districts, as well as private schools, prefer to hire teachers who have some experience with the special population they will be teaching.

Advancement to supervisor, principal, or a higher position is difficult and very slow. In all government and public school positions you will need additional coursework and experience in order to qualify for certification in the state in which you are working. Promotions to higher administrative positions usually require you to have a Ph.D. or Ed.D. degree and many years of experience in the field.

At the state and federal government level, teachers may qualify for administrative, adult training, and vocational counseling positions within human service and education departments.

Employment Outlook

Salaries for beginning special education teachers in public schools range from $10,000 to $12,000 for a nine-month or ten-month year depending on geographic location. School systems in large cities may offer several thousand more. Private schools, on the other hand, may offer considerably less with starting salaries often as low as $9000 with a B.A. and state certification. In the past few years, however, private schools have begun to compete more favorably with the public sector and to offer other benefits such as health and dental plans.

State institutions and private residential schools offer higher salaries for a 12-month year. The starting range generally falls between $12,000 and $15,000 with private schools paying the lower figure.

Supervisory positions vary greatly depending, again, on whether the job is in the public or private sector, the location of the school, and the experience and degree required for the position. The average salary for a supervisor with five years of supervisory experience is $24,000.

Additional Information

Individual state departments of education must be contacted to find out if you qualify for certification in that state. A fee is usually required to have your credentials evaluated. Information may also be gathered by contacting the following sources:

Bureau of Education for the Handicapped
Department of Health, Education, and Welfare
Washington, DC 20201

U.S. Department of Education
400 Maryland Avenue, SW
Washington, DC 20202

National Education Association
1201 16th Street, NW
Washington, DC 20036

References

Harshman, H., (Ed.). *Educating the Emotionally Disturbed.* Thomas Y. Crowell Co., 1969.

Kirk, Samuel. *Educating Exceptional Children.* Houghton Mifflin Co., 1972.

Long, J., Morse, W., and Newman, R. *Conflict in the Classroom: The Education of Emotionally Disturbed Children.* 3rd ed., Wadsworth Publishing Co., Inc., 1976.

Newcomer, P.L. *Understanding and Teaching Emotionally Disturbed Children.* Allyn and Bacon, Inc., 1980.

Popovich, D., and Laham, S. *The Adaptive Behavior Curriculum.* Vols. 1 & 2, Paul H. Brookes Publishing Co., Inc., 1981/1982.

Wallace, G., and McLaughlin, J. *Learning Disabilities; Concepts and Characteristics.* Charles E. Merrill Publishing Co., 1975.

Nursing

Training, Technique, and Tenderness

"Are you there Nurse?"

In the hushed and darkened hospital room the voice of the elderly woman sounds fragile and very afraid.

"Yes, I'm right here," you answer reassuringly. "Is there something you would like me to do?"

"Not really. It's just so quiet in here. I thought maybe I was all alone." Mrs. Johnson's voice becomes apologetic as she adds: "I'm sorry to be such a bother to you. I don't know what's come over me these days."

"You're no bother at all, Mrs. Johnson," you declare cheerfully. "And if there's anything you want, please go right ahead and ask. That's what I'm here for, you know."

"I just can't seem to go to sleep. I know that medication you gave me was supposed to make me sleepy but my thoughts keep going around and around inside my head."

Her voice has a slight catch in it as she continues: "I feel as if I'm getting to be so much trouble for everyone. I mean with all those tests and questions Dr. Whelan and that other doctor too, you know . . . that anesthetist keep doing . . . and all the other things you nurses have to do to get me ready for tomorrow. I feel like you're taking a lot of time with me."

Turning on the light by the bed, you search for the right words to alleviate Mrs. Johnson's mounting anxiety.

"Dr. Whelan is a very careful surgeon and so is Dr. Smith, the anesthetist who asked you those questions this evening. They both want to know just as much about you as they can before the operation so that they will be totally prepared and there won't be any problems," you explain seriously. "That's why they do all that blood work and even the tests you had before you came to the hospital."

"Dr. Whelan certainly seems to be thorough," Mrs. Johnson agrees. "My son says he's one of the best internists in the state."

"I'm sure your son is right," you say positively. "I know he has an excellent reputation here."

"I just wonder if, maybe, I'm not too old for this kind of thing. It's so very expensive to be here and . . ." Mrs. Johnson's pale blue eyes brim with tears as she continues, ". . . and it might be such a waste of time and money anyway."

Affecting an attitude of mock indignation, you declare firmly: "Mrs. Johnson, do you believe for one minute that Dr. Whelan would put you through this operation if he was at all worried about your recovery? Do you honestly think he wants to ruin his fine record? He wants to have another healthy patient telling all her friends how wonderful he is!

"And besides that," you continue sternly, "you are a very, very special person to your family. Whatever this operation costs doesn't even begin to compare with what you mean to your children and their families." Softening your voice a bit, you add, "I think you know that already, don't you?"

"You're right," she murmurs. "I guess I'm being foolish to be so worried.

"Would you sit here and talk to me for a while," she asks, "just until I start to feel sleepy? Would you tell me some more about your daughter's graduation? It sounds like you had such a happy time."

You pull your chair close to the bed and there, at one o'clock in the morning, you sit with this tiny, frightened lady. As you describe your weekend, you are helping to ease her terror over tomorrow's surgery in the most effective way you know. By sharing your pleasure over this special family event, you help her feel that she is also special to you. And while you chat companionably about the springtime loveliness of the campus and your pride in your daughter, you observe Mrs. Johnson begin to relax and then, finally, to fall asleep.

Even though each patient is different and each situation is unique, you have learned that discussing ordinary things in your everyday life often seems to help frightened people feel calmer. When you stay close by, patients, especially children and frail and gentle people like Mrs. Johnson, relax better and sleep more soundly than when they are alone in a hospital room.

Each time you show more care and attention than is expected, such as arranging cards nearby, plumping up the pillows, explaining the medical procedures you have to perform, keeping a lighthearted attitude, and a number of other considerations and attentions, you know that your patient usually senses that you wish her well.

It is not always easy to be a nurse, you think with a sigh, because many patients are not as sweet and friendly as Mrs. Johnson, and you are usually much busier than you are tonight. But each day is a new challenge, testing your knowledge as well as your stamina.

As a private duty nurse, your job differs from that of the nurses employed directly by the hospital. The nurse on the ward is responsible for the medical care and attention to all of the patients in her section. She generally has no time to spend sitting with any one patient while on duty. You, on the other hand, are employed by a patient or a family in order to assure that all of your time will be spent taking care of that one patient. Usually, the person you are caring for is very ill and needs constant attention.

You may, as in Mrs. Johnson's case, be hired to see a patient through the critical stages of an operation. You may be required to provide constant attention to a person whose illness is terminal. Or you may be hired to work, not in a hospital or a nursing home, but in the patient's home. This usually occurs when a person is very ill but does not need to be hospitalized.

There are times when you miss the bustle and excitement of the days when you were working as part of the hospital staff. Shifts were long and demanding of your energy and your skill but you certainly felt vital and enthusiastic.

Working in the hospital also kept your training ongoing as you constantly learned new techniques and utilized updated equipment. The professional contact with the doctors and other nurses was also exhilarating most of the time.

In private duty the pace is usually calmer and you have to take more personal responsibility for keeping your skills up-to-date, but you have the chance to know your patient better. You are right there whenever you are needed and do not have to rush off to tend to someone else at a crucial time. You often feel the satisfaction of knowing that your expert care played a large part in a person's recovery.

Another advantage for you, right now, is that you have more opportunity for selecting the shift that is best for your lifestyle. This is a reason why many married women who have children choose private duty nursing as a career.

Where Do Nurses Work?

A nursing career can take many directions. Most nurses are employed in hospitals. They may work in a ward where all of the patients need one type of care, such as a pediatric ward, psychiatric ward, or cardiac ward, or they may work on a floor with post-operative patients, people needing intensive care, in the emergency room, or, as in the case of urban areas, in a trauma section.

Nurses may also be employed directly by doctors in offices where they perform routine laboratory and office work as well as nursing services. They may work in schools, factories, and large corporations.

A large number of nurses are employed by public and private health care agencies such as neighborhood clinics and visiting nurse services.

Nurses may teach in colleges and may also conduct community training courses in communicable diseases, prenatal care, sex education, mental health, and other public health services.

Federal, state, and local agencies hire nurses. Private agencies, nursing homes, sanatoriums, and boarding schools also employ nurses. The armed forces train and hire nurses.

Although nursing is not a high-salaried profession, there is always a need for qualified nurses. Opportunities exist throughout the country for both registered and practical nurses.

Nursing has always been a very important branch of the network of human services. Every clinic, agency, community center, day-care center, nursing home, and visiting home service, whether public or private, large or small, urban or rural, has nurses on staff or on call.

A young man who has just moved from a mental institution to a new life in a halfway house may need nurses to help him understand how to regulate his medication. A physically disabled woman, learning to care for her own needs, will need a nurse to visit regularly to check her progress. A profoundly retarded person who needs total care in an institution will have to have constant nursing services. A hospitalized alcoholic also may need round-the-clock nursing in order to help restore his health. An elderly couple trying to maintain dignity and independence as long as possible will need visiting nurse services.

Nurses in neighborhood clinics may be engaged in large scale immunization programs, prenatal care classes, and many other health care projects for people who are not able to afford private medical services.

Public health nurses must possess the same ability to follow orders precisely, react efficiently in emergencies, and cope with human pain and suffering as other nurses do. They also may be responsible for follow-up treatments and home visits.

Nurses who work in institutions attend to problems which involve feeding and sleeping patterns, diet, toilet care, and other aspects of routine living. They must be concerned with contributing to program development in self-help areas and consulting with professionals in other disciplines as well.

Usually, major nursing functions can be described as treatment, prevention, and casefinding. All of these functions will overlap to some extent. The nurse who works in a private or public residential facility will be primarily concerned with treatment whether the clients are developmentally disabled, physically disabled, or mentally ill.

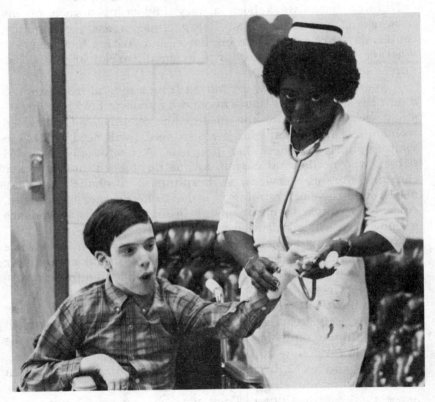

Direct patient contact is the most gratifying aspect of nursing. (Photo by Marlene Wiener, courtesy of Woodbridge State School)

Nurses who work in the community in human service areas will probably be very involved with programs to prevent problems from starting. They may be working to publicize the dangers to infants of poisoning from lead paint or the danger to unborn babies if the mothers are exposed to rubella, alcoholism, or drug addiction. They may also be actively searching to find cases that can be helped with early diagnosis and treatment of health problems.

In small agencies or in rural areas, the nurse may be the only full-time professional and is called upon to carry out duties that normally belong to social workers, therapists, and administrators. One of the nurse's most important responsibilities, in that case, is to have as thorough a knowledge as possible of where to refer clients for the proper solution of their problems.

Private duty nurses (registered nurses and licensed practical nurses) often play an important role in meeting human service needs. Frequently, they provide home care to the sick and the feeble at the request of a government health program. They may also work in nursing homes when a patient needs more than just the routine care provided by the home.

Psychiatric nurses provide a very specialized service, often in institutional or residential settings. These nurses are highly trained.

Qualifications and Education

Registered nurses (R.N.s) may become qualified by:

1. Attending a two-year program at a junior or community college.

2. Attending a qualified nursing school program. This may be a three-year program.

3. Graduation from a four-year college with a B.A. degree in nursing. Registration must be granted by the state in which you are nursing. Public health and school nurses generally must have a B.A. degree.

Licensed practical nurses (L.P.N.s) must have attended a one-year, state-approved program offered by a junior or community college, trade or technical school, local hospital, health agency, or private school. The U.S. Army also has a training program which is approved by the states.

Advancement as an L.P.N. is limited without formal education. Many hospitals have training programs that assist in completing requirements for the R.N. certificate while working part-time as an L.P.N.

R.N.s may become head nurses or directors of nursing services but these positions usually require a B.A. degree or higher.

Employment Outlook

R.N.s working in hospitals average between $13,000 and $17,000 per year. If you work in a nursing home or for a private physician, your salary may be less while government agencies and industry may pay slightly more. Salaries throughout the country range from $12,000 to $22,000 depending on geographical location, urban or rural position, and years of experience.

L.P.N. positions average about $11,000 per year. A large proportion of L.P.N.s, however, work part-time or privately and are therefore paid by the hour or the day.

Private duty nurses are paid at a daily rate which varies greatly, depending on the position, its location, and whether you are an R.N. or an L.P.N. The daily rate for R.N.s may range from $50.00 up to $100.00. L.P.N.s may earn from $25.00 to $60.00 per day.

Additional Information

For additional information about career opportunities in nursing contact:

Department of Nursing Education
American Nurses Association
2420 Pershing Road
Kansas City, MO 64108

Career Information Service
National League for Nursing
10 Columbus Circle
New York, NY 10019

National Association for Practical Nurse Education
  and Service, Inc.
122 East 42nd Street
New York, NY 10019

References

Balthazar, E., and Stevens, H. *The Emotionally Disturbed, Mentally Retarded: A Historical Contemporary Perspective.* Prentice-Hall, Inc., 1975.

Baskin, D. "Mental Health Systems and Services in the United States." *Journal of Mental Health Administration.* Vol. 8, No. 2, Fall 1981.

Frederickson, K. *Opportunities in Nursing.* National Textbook Co., 1977.

Holmes, M., and Holmes, D. *Handbook of Human Services for Older Persons.* Human Sciences Press, 1979.

Magreb, P., and Elder, J. *Planning for Services to Handicapped Persons: Community, Education, Health.* Paul H. Brookes Publishing Co., Inc., 1979.

Schwartz, H. *The Case for American Medicine; A Realistic Look at Our Health Care System.* McKay, 1972.

Nutrition

Dieticians and nutritionists are not usually included in listings of human service professionals in spite of the fact that many of them are employed by human service agencies and organizations in many different capacities.

The dietician in today's world is a professional who is directly involved with helping to solve some of the major problems of society. The scope of the field of nutrition has expanded enormously in the last two decades. It is providing many new opportunities to people who are trained in this interesting field. In this section you will read about some of the important concerns of the nutritionist as well as some of the interesting places that people in this field work.

Dietetics has become a career area that is exciting, rewarding, and holds great promise for people interested in being where the action is. Across the nation, dieticians are being called upon to assume greater responsibilities than ever before. Scientific research is determining how food influences our health, vitality, longevity, and even our personality.

As the world seems to grow smaller and hungry mouths increase, we must persist in the search for improving ways of feeding the needy. Nutritional science plays as large a part in that search as agriculture and agribusiness do.

In the medical arena, it is recognized that proper nutrition can prevent disease and help to alleviate many health problems. The importance of nutrition for pregnant women and for the optimum development of children is greatly stressed. There is also a growing awareness of the special nutritional needs of the elderly. Our increasingly sedentary mode of life has changed our nutritional needs, but our eating habits are not keeping pace with those changes.

The dietician is assuming increasing importance as the professional responsible for the knowledge and practice of nutritional care. Registered dieticians are trained in biological science, behavioral science, management systems, and, most importantly, food and food science. Because of the enormous range in the practice of dietetics, the educational program of the dietician is rigorous and broad.

A dietician must be well-trained in understanding, interpreting, and determining the nutritional needs of a person depending upon his physical condition at the time. The dietician must be able to research his patient's eating habits, background, economic situation—all of the other factors which make the patient what he is. Then the dietician must draw up a nutritional program that fits the patient's budget and suits his cultural palate to either correct nutritional deficits or maintain good health.

What Do Dieticians Do?

Dieticians are called upon to perform many interesting and demanding roles in the human services. Due to the nature of the population you are serving, or the location of the agency or hospital where you are working, you might be found in any of the following situations as a dietician:

- As a consultant on a hospital health care team, your responsibilities would include careful study of a patient's physical structure, general nutritional needs, and specific acute care situations. You would then be called upon to make important recommendations for his nutritional care, which may include some sort of therapy.

- A small child may be critically ill as the result of burns from an automobile accident. Your job would include designing a nutritional program for him which will include massive nutrient feeding to insure the best chance for survival.

- As the dietician in the maximum care section of an institution for the profoundly retarded, you may be called upon to design a festive picnic for 50 clients who are able to eat only pureed food.

- Working in a daytime recreation center for the elderly population in an inner-city area, you would have to set up lunch programs providing sound nutrition, tastiness, and eye appeal, probably on a totally inadequate budget.

- As a private practitioner counseling a new diabetic in the necessity of careful diet and weight control, it would be your job to provide a diet that carefully monitors sugar intake while balancing all the essential nutritional needs of the patient.

- In schools you may be employed full-time to design the day-to-day nutritional program and to teach good eating habits to disadvantaged children.

- In residential care facilities you may have to check temperatures and monitor the service of food to clients to insure that all food is properly prepared and maintained in a wholesome condition from the time it leaves the supplier until it is consumed.

- You may be called upon to investigate the nutritive content of a client's diet in order to identify the cause of a deteriorating physical condition due to improper diet.

- Working for a community health program you may be asked to plan a meaningful city-wide program to highlight a "Good Nutrition Week" campaign through school contests, radio and television publicity, and a pamphlet distribution program which teaches proper nutrition in a cartoon-like layout.

Where Do Dieticians Work?

Although most people tend to picture dieticians as working in hospitals and other institutions, they are found in industry, food processing plants, universities, community agencies, and wherever nutritional advice and care is part of the job. In addition to their primary responsibilities as nutritional experts, most dieticians also function as managers and as teachers.

In health care facilities, the dietetics department is generally one of the largest departments and its budget is equally formidable. The dieticians are charged with the responsibility of turning large-scale feeding of less-than-healthy individuals into a nutritionally sound and socially or emotionally pleasant interlude.

As a member of a community care team, dieticians help to plan and coordinate the nutritional aspects of all programs designed to improve or prevent existing health problems. They may work in day-care centers, community or municipal agencies, state or other government departments, or other public health facilities.

If you are in private practice you may be working in a wide variety of situations. You will be called upon to give advice to individuals, schools, or businesses concerning nutrition, food preparation, and service. You may provide advice and service to nursing homes, private hospitals, clinics, and restaurants.

As part of management in most facilities, you will be responsible for planning, directing, organizing, and assessing programs of food preparation and service. You will have to establish and maintain standards, hire, train, and supervise

Dietary/nutrition supervisors may train and assist new food service staff. (Photo by Marlene Wiener)

personnel, and give in-service training programs. You will also have to plan for and then work within budgetary limitations.

Another important role for dieticians today is that of formally or informally educating the public about the crucial relationship of nutrition with many of the economic, scientific, and even political issues which are being dealt with in large and small ways. Dieticians teach in colleges and universities, nursing schools and other health-related educational programs, and technical schools. They are also called upon to lecture and to give demonstrations to public and private service organizations as well as to high schools and businesses. Industries also utilize dieticians for educating personnel who deal with aspects of food preparation, distribution, or purchase.

How to Become a Registered Dietician

It is very helpful to have a good background in chemistry, biology, and mathematics. Additional college courses in business, marketing, health, and psychology will also be useful.

To become a registered dietician you must meet the following requirements established by the American Dietetic Association: completion of an approved curriculum leading to a bachelor's degree plus qualifying experience which is available through an accredited, coordinated undergraduate program combining coursework and supervised experience; or an accredited dietetic internship in a health care facility, college, or school; or a three-year, pre-approved work experience preceded by associate membership in the A.D.A.; or an advanced degree in nutrition or related areas with a six-month, full-time, pre-approved qualifying experience.

Once the requirements are met, you are eligible to take the national registration examination. Continuing education requirements are necessary to maintain registered dietician status.

Employment Opportunities

Advancement opportunities are excellent and career mobility is facilitated as nutritionists become more involved with physical fitness, weight control, and national health problems. Each day there seem to be more opportunities to use a background in nutrition in the development and selling of food products as well as nutrition programs.

Nutritionists who reach the master's or Ph.D. level may teach at the college or university level in all programs involving health care. They also are in demand for administrative positions in health facilities and in government positions.

Beginning dieticians may earn about $13,000 per year, particularly in smaller communities. Experienced dieticians are now earning from $15,000 to $30,000 per year depending on years in service and additional education.

Additional Information

Information on internship programs, educational developments, and employment opportunities may be obtained by contacting:

The American Dietetic Association
430 North Michigan Avenue
Chicago, IL 60611

Society for Nutrition Education
1736 Franklin Street
Oakland, CA 94612

A list of universities that offer graduate programs in nutrition may be obtained by writing to:

American Institute of Nutrition
9650 Rockville Pike
Bethesda, MD 20814

References

American Dietetic Association. *Dieticians: The Professionals in Nutritional Care*, 1981.

Levinson, J. "Nutrition Forecast: Food for Thought," in *Health Care Employment*. New York Times, 1982.

Magreb, P., and Elder, J. *Planning for Services to Handicapped Persons: Community, Education, Health*. Paul H. Brookes Publishing Co., Inc., 1979.

Norback, C.T. *Careers Encyclopedia*. Dow Jones-Irwin, 1980.

3. THE VITAL THERAPIES

Speech Therapy, Physical Therapy, Occupational Therapy, and Art, Music, and Dance Therapy

Therapists treat disabilities. They test to determine the need for treatment, plan a program of graduated treatment, and administer treatment designed to restore or improve the affected ability. Therapists are also frequently called upon to design, build, or repair some of the equipment they use in providing treatment. Whereas social workers, teachers, nurses, and nutritionists work to improve the social and physical conditions of people by providing habilitative, educational, medical, and community services, the therapist deals specifically with the part of a person that is disabled.

The psychotherapist, as mentioned earlier, performs this function and so do professionals in some relatively new areas. They are grouped together in this section because many of the services they provide are interrelated.

The therapies discussed in this chapter are probably the best career choices in human services today. They are all expanding in this age of technology. New scientific discoveries are constantly improving treatment methods and increasing the scope of knowledge within each area. This is reflected in the growing demand for services and the ease of job mobility within each profession.

One of the oldest and most established of the therapies is speech therapy. Audiologists and speech pathologists evaluate, test, and treat speech and hearing disorders.

Audiologists test and work with people who have hearing problems. Speech pathologists work to help clients who have speech, voice, or language disorders. These may be the result of many conditions such as brain injury, hearing loss, mental retardation, emotional disorders, or cleft palate. Speech pathologists also work with individuals who wish to change or improve their ways of speaking.

Another important profession in the human services is physical therapy. This field deals with people whose disabilities are the result of accidents, strokes, arthritis or other crippling diseases, paralysis, or amputations.

Physical therapists work closely with physicians and other specialists. They test the patient and then create a program of exercise, massage, and any other therapeutic treatment that will relieve pain and restore or improve muscular strength or range of motion.

One of the fastest growing employment areas is occupational therapy. If you choose this profession, you might work with mentally, physically, or emotionally disabled people of all ages. You will help them to regain their original functioning level if they are suffering from severe emotional breakdowns or will help other clients develop skills to move towards greater physical, social, and even financial independence.

You will plan and carry out a program of vocational, educational, and recreational activities. You may teach weaving, ceramics, needlework, or carpentry. You may adapt games and recreational activities to meet the needs of handicapped individuals. You may also be called upon to design and even make special equipment to aid clients in working or improving mobility in playing games.

Music, art, and dance therapy are often grouped together and termed the "expressive therapies." They are the newest of the recognized therapy areas, although, for many years, psychologists and teachers have been aware of their value in programs leading to sound mental health. They are still so new that they are not rigidly defined and their boundaries overlap with each other and with other disciplines.

Essentially, therapists in these areas help people to learn to express themselves and to communicate with others through nonverbal outlets. They focus on the development of improved self-image and awareness of a person's feelings about himself and the world within which he moves and reacts.

As therapies, music, art, and dance share many common goals, but they demand initial expertise in very different and demanding artistic areas.

Each of the six careers in this section focuses on improving the quality of life enjoyed by people who are disabled in one way or another. They don't deal with improving or changing the environment but rather with the client's ability to act or interact with that environment.

Speech Therapy and Audiology

Speaking Easy

This is going to be a long day, you decide after glancing at your schedule. Today you will be testing a group of children who are not only severely retarded, but also blind and, perhaps, deaf. As staff audiologist in this state institution, you are required to test the hearing of its 700 developmentally disabled residents yearly. You also spend three days each week working directly with deaf/blind clients. You have been working with the seven children on today's schedule for a number of years.

The institution's speech department is relatively large, now that it has become an Intermediate Care Facility (I.C.F.) and, therefore, eligible for federal assistance. There are 15 speech therapists working under a Director of Speech Therapies. This is a far cry from four short years ago when you and two aides attempted to handle the speech and hearing needs of the 1000 people who then lived in the institution.

Although your department is still understaffed and the clients would certainly profit from additional services, many children and adults are involved in new and effective programs. Electronic communication boards and other advancements in technology have opened up new worlds for the speech and hearing impaired. The progress of some residents undergoing regularly scheduled and intensive speech therapy has been remarkable. Many clients have qualified for placements in more advanced schools for the deaf.

Ironically, the main reason that made you choose to work here eight years ago—the tremendous variety of speech and hearing disorders found in this multiply handicapped population—was the same reason that nearly made you leave six years later.

It was exciting at first to deal with the complex problems of so many children and adults. There were residents with hearing losses, cleft palates, no apparent ability to communicate, severe eating problems, interesting and often very rare syndromes, speech problems due to Down's Syndrome, cerebral palsy, and all sorts of other disabilities. But after several years, challenge turned to frustration. Each resident tested and problem identified meant one more person for whom you would write a treatment program that you never had time to carry out.

"Well, that's all changed now," you tell yourself with satisfaction. Meeting the standards necessary in order to maintain I.C.F. status has not been easy. In fact it takes constant self-monitoring and evaluation in order to pass the rigorous standards of the auditing team. But the hard work is paying off. All of the higher functioning clients have long since moved out of the institution to, hopefully, less restrictive environments. And the residents now active in programs all over the grounds are people who received little or no individual attention in earlier days.

A noise in the hallway interrupts your train of thought and reminds you that your first client is arriving. It is time to stop daydreaming and to go to work.

As you glance out of your office door, you observe Jimmy Cotton sitting listlessly in his wheelchair. He looks so young and fragile that he seems much younger than his 17 years.

Sally, the attendant who brought him over from the dormitory, is an old friend of yours and she smiles warmly as she says: "Here's Jimmy for you. He might need to have his ears cleaned again. He's been rubbing and scratching at them something fierce! Dr. Young checked him over yesterday and he doesn't seem to have an infection, but he acts as if they're bothering him."

"Okay Jimmy," you say, touching him reassuringly on the arm so that he will know you are there. "Let's look inside those ears. Maybe we can find something interesting in there."

As Sally sits down to wait on a bench in the hallway, you wheel Jimmy into the office. Because he cannot see and has been classified as deaf, you spend a little time helping him to orient himself by letting him touch you and the desk top nearby. You stand fairly close to him so that he may be able to sense your nearness and smell your cologne. Most of your actions are part of a well-established routine.

With your otoscope, you carefully look into Jimmy's right ear. "Aha!" you say out loud. "Potatoes! You could grow potatoes in that ear, my friend." From the hall you can hear Sally laugh.

That's one of your favorite lines, and children who can hear and understand seem to look forward to the long list of vegetables you pretend to see as you look through the otoscope. Even when a client is deaf and blind, your silly behavior often gets picked up and he will demonstrate amusement by smiling delightedly or by giggling. This time, however, Jimmy continues to look placid and uninvolved.

You finish checking his ears, noting the information carefully and making an appointment for the doctor to clean his ears next week. Then you wheel Jimmy into the small blue soundproof room built into a corner of the office. Now you will attempt to test his hearing.

Inside the booth, you position Jimmy so that he is facing a small window that looks out on the office. There is a table just in front of the window upon which are several small wooden blocks and an empty cigar box.

Very gently, you bring his hands to the table and help him to feel the blocks. You also place one of his hands in the box to show him that it is there.

To the side of the table, there is a set of earphones hanging on the wall. You place them, for a moment, in Jimmy's hands to let him feel them. Then you place them on his head. Very cautiously, he reaches up to touch them but he does not try to take them off.

Although Jimmy is legally deaf and blind, like most people in this category, he is not totally deaf. Other clients in the program have some vision too, but not Jimmy.

Often, when a child is deaf and blind, the sensory deprivation will cause him to appear more retarded than he actually is. Therefore, careful testing is vital to devise the best treatment and program for them. Jimmy's teacher and his assigned speech therapist have worked closely to teach him sorting skills. He is now able to feel the difference between square and round shapes and to sort them into two boxes. You will utilize this important skill to test his hearing.

Once Jimmy is settled and you are sure that he knows what to do, you step outside the booth and close the door. The audiometer is on the outside of the booth, just under the window. Sitting down in front of it, you carefully adjust the dials which regulate the frequency and the volume.

Through the window, you can see Jimmy sitting in front of you. He is carefully feeling his headphones and you hope that he keeps them in place during the testing session.

The electric pure-tone audiometer is one of the most accurate methods of testing since it produces pure tones of known intensity and frequency which are necessary for evaluating hearing. Frequency refers to the number of vibrations, or cycles, per second of a given sound wave. The higher the pitch of the sound, the greater the frequency. A person might not be able to hear sounds at certain frequencies while having no difficulty at all at frequencies that are higher, lower, or in between. Intensity refers to the loudness of the sound. The most important frequencies for the understanding of speech range between 500 and 2000 vibrations per second.

To find a person's hearing level it is necessary to determine what intensity of sound is necessary for him to hear at each of the frequencies. The audiometer presents the client with sounds of known intensity and frequency and asks him to respond when he hears the tone. The degree of hearing loss is then recorded on an audiogram.

Routine audiometric procedures cannot always be used with infants, small children, some psychotic patients, and the severely mentally retarded because they will not respond reliably to instructions. Clinical evaluation of these groups can be accomplished by electrodermal testing and other procedures, such as E.E.G. (electroencephalogram) audiometry and operant conditioning audiometry. The last procedure is the one you are now using with Jimmy.

Setting the dials carefully, you begin to test. Again and again you press the sound button but Jimmy sits calmly inside, apparently unaware of any noise. Then, at 125 cycles, you observe that he becomes alert. Very slowly he picks up a block and puts it into the box. His brow furrows in concentration. He has heard something. You press the tone again and he puts another block next to the first one.

As you mark his responses on the audiogram, you recall the first time Jimmy responded to sound for you. You had been trying for a long time to devise a way to test him accurately. He had demonstrated no hearing at all, even at 1000 cycles, and yet his day-to-day responses indicated that he seemed to be hearing something. Then, when you set the audiometer at 125 cycles per second, he responded.

That was a moment that you will always remember.

What Do Speech Therapists and Audiologists Do?

The speech therapist is a very important member of any human service treatment team. A career in this field would enable you to perform an enormous range of services for many different populations. It is one of the most technical human service careers and requires very specialized training. Among the variety of possible jobs, you might:

- help deaf children develop speech and language, use hearing aids, and learn speechreading

- teach people with cerebral palsy to use electronic communication boards to enhance their ability to work and socialize with others

- assist stroke or accident victims regain speech

- help profoundly retarded children develop better feeding skills

- work with people who have severe stuttering problems

- teach sign language and fingerspelling

- work with children who suffer from cleft palate

- provide voice therapy to change someone's pitch

- remedy articulation problems in schoolchildren

- work with autistic or emotionally disturbed children

Patience is an extremely important attribute for speech therapists since their clients' progress is generally slow. An audiologist or speech pathologist must be able to establish the kind of rapport that will encourage and motivate very depressed or angry clients. Speech therapists must also be able to maintain an objective viewpoint and be good at working with detail.

Speech therapy and audiology are so interrelated that training and experience in one field requires a thorough background in the other.

Where Do Speech Therapists Work?

Most speech therapists work in public or private schools, the places where speech and hearing problems first begin to interfere with a child's progress. Also, since many speech and hearing disabilities are not severe, they can often be worked with in a public school setting.

Many audiologists and speech pathologists work in colleges and universities where they teach and do research. Others work in hospitals, clinics, industry, and private practice. The government employs a large number of therapists in state and federal agencies, veterans hospitals, institutions for the retarded and the mentally ill, and in public schools and institutes for the deaf.

This is a growing field because of the established recognition and diagnosis of speech and hearing problems in children. New

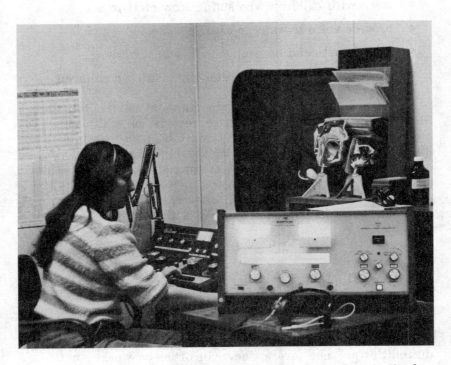

The audiologist's careful assessment of hearing disorders is the key to effective treatment programs. (Photo by Maurya Farah)

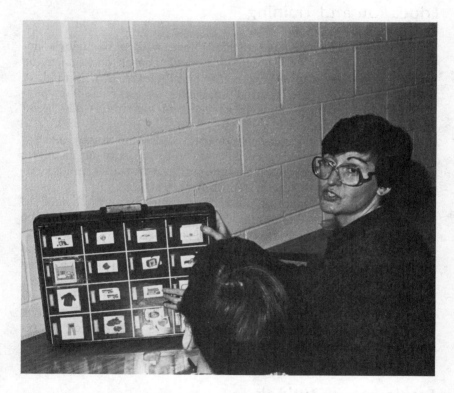

A speech pathologist improves communication skills in a nonverbal client by using an electronic language board. (Photo by Carrington Brown, courtesy of Woodbridge State School)

laws which require services for handicapped children as well as programs for the aged and indigent through Medicare and Medicaid have resulted in many new jobs in speech therapy.

Competition for jobs is keen, particularly in large urban areas, but opportunities are good in smaller cities and towns.

Most positions, except those at entry-level, require graduate degrees.

Education and Training

Graduation from an accredited college with a bachelor's degree in speech therapy, speech pathology, speech correction, or hearing disorders is a minimum for employment in this field. A bachelor's degree in a related field such as education or psychology plus graduate work in speech and hearing is also good career preparation.

Most jobs require a master's degree, and some states also require you to have teaching certificates in order to teach in public schools. Graduate programs include advanced studies in specialized areas as well as supervised clinical training.

In order to gain professional advancement you will need to secure a Certificate of Clinical Competence (C.C.C.) from the American Speech and Hearing Association. This is granted to those who have a master's degree or the equivalent, who have completed a one-year internship, and who pass a written examination.

In 29 states, speech pathologists, therapists, and audiologists must be licensed if they practice outside of school situations. The state Department of Education will provide information on requirements necessary for becoming licensed.

Employment Outlook

Starting salaries in government positions for therapists with master's degrees or one year of professional experience are about $15,000. Average salaries in public school or government positions for experienced therapists are about $24,000 (much higher if you have a Ph.D.).

In urban areas, salaries for nongovernment positions are often much higher, particularly for therapists in private practice.

Additional Information

Additional information can be obtained by writing to:

American Speech and Hearing Association
9030 Old Georgetown Road
Washington, DC 20014

References

Delacato, C. *The Diagnosis and Treatment of Speech and Reading Problems*. Charles C. Thomas, 1963.

Kirk, S. *Educating Exceptional Children*. Houghton Mifflin Co., 1972.

Magreb, P., and Elder, J. *Planning for Services to Handicapped Persons: Community, Education, Health*. Paul H. Brookes Publishing Co., Inc., 1979.

Travis, L.E. (Ed.). *Handbook of Speech Pathology*. Appleton-Century-Crofts, 1957.

Van Riper, C. *A Career in Speech Pathology*. Prentice-Hall, Inc., 1979.

Van Riper, C. *Speech Correction: Principles and Methods*. 6th ed. Prentice-Hall, Inc., 1978.

Physical Therapy

Easy Does It

The large double glass doors slide open noiselessly on their tracks as you enter the physical therapy wing of the hospital. They are newly installed and very expensive for the facility, but you and the rest of the staff campaigned hard for their purchase and installation. Their value is brought home to all of you every time you watch a patient using crutches or a walker easily enter the building. The accessibility of the building and its various therapy rooms have been markedly improved for patients and their families, and this has far-reaching psychological implications for people suffering from physical disabilities.

It was so difficult for some of your patients to get into the building before the renovations that they were often frustrated and exhausted at the beginning of the therapy session. Non-disabled people, you reflect, have no conception of the stress and anxiety experienced by handicapped people as they attempt to live a normal life. Stepping up one or two steps to enter a building, something not even noticed by most people as they move in and out of homes, offices, and restaurants, are just like a **DO NOT ENTER** sign to a person in a wheelchair. Some doorknobs and heavy, self-closing doors are impossible for people to negotiate when they suffer from debilitating disorders like arthritis or crippling conditions stemming from cerebral palsy, strokes, or accidents. Narrow doorways, halls with no railings, and bathroom stalls too small to admit wheelchairs are only some of the constant problems encountered by disabled people every day and in nearly every environment.

As you flick the light switch, the large therapy room is flooded with bright fluorescent light. The shiny equipment looks awkward and otherworldly in the empty room. Leg braces hang stiffly on their hooks. Metal walkers are stacked neatly, like summer furniture, against the far wall. Large, colorful geometric shapes made of foam rubber are piled in a corner like building blocks for giant children. Later, when they are used for positioning and exercising, they will not seem so strange to the eye.

There are parallel bars for walking and steps for climbing. Pulleys, mats, and weights all sit quietly, waiting for the day to begin.

Much of your equipment is old and somewhat outdated. It was purchased years ago or donated, already well-used, by more affluent hospitals and clinics. The renovation money did stretch, however, to include a small all-purpose workshop where minor adjustments and adaptations to equipment can be designed and made. In addition, it paid for the new hydrotherapy equipment in the room across the hall. Hydrotherapy, the medicinal use of water, is of great benefit to the healing and providing relief from pain of certain diseases and injuries. Depending on the treatment plan, the patient may be treated with cold water, warm water, alternating cold and warm water, or with still or moving water.

Off to the side of the room are four small cubicles which serve as offices for the therapists on staff. Yours has a tiny desk piled high with the paperwork which you are coming in early to complete.

On the opposite side of the room are two doors leading to the conference rooms where you and the other therapists meet with families and patients to evaluate progress, discuss problems, and plan for future treatments.

The back of the room is mirrored like a dance studio so that your patients can observe themselves as they move. A gently inclined ramp with railings is directly in front of the mirrors, as well as two stationary bicycles.

Your monthly reports are due tomorrow and you have yet to correlate the results of the last three tests you administered yesterday. In addition, you are meeting with Dr. Williams at ten o'clock to discuss Karen's worsening scoliosis. As a physiatrist, a physician who specializes in physical medicine, he will advise you about the best course of treatment to prevent further deformity of her spine. You also expect Philip to stop by. He is the prosthetist who makes most of the braces that you use.

Then, at 11 o'clock, you are seeing a new patient. Your records show that he is a young man suffering the after effects of a massive hemorrhage to the brain. Since you have not seen him yet, you have not formulated any treatment plan, but the preliminary reports sent by the doctor lead you to believe that the young man will be able to make a successful recovery.

Another busy day, you reflect eagerly, as you head toward your monthly reports.

Why Be a Physical Therapist?

Physical therapy is an excellent career choice if you are someone who will enjoy helping people who have physical disabilities. You will be working closely with physicians and other specialists in order to design and implement rehabilitative programs of exercise, massage, or therapeutic treatment.

You will be working to improve muscle conditions resulting from many physical causes. You also will attempt to maintain muscle tone in limbs that are paralyzed. In addition to massage, you will use cold treatments to reduce conditions of swelling and heat treatments to relieve pain.

It will be your responsibility to design programs of exercise using many different kinds of equipment such as pulleys, weights, stationary bicycles, parallel bars, and all sorts of mats, standing tables, walkers, and positioning materials.

Improvements in technology have produced such therapeutic advances as whirlpool treatments, ultrasonic machinery, ultraviolet and infrared lamps. All of these medical wonders assist you in helping patients to cope with pain and disability.

Part of your job will be teaching patients and their families to use and care for wheelchairs, braces, crutches, and artificial limbs.

Where Do Physical Therapists Work?

Although hospitals employ the greatest number of physical therapists, there are also career opportunities in public health agencies, rehabilitation centers, schools for handicapped children, and private and public service agencies for the aged or disabled. You may prefer to work with one particular group of clients, such as children who have arthritis or cerebral palsy, or you may wish to specialize in treatments for stroke victims or people with paralyzing conditions. If you work for a large hospital or clinic, you may be treating a wide range of people needing a variety of therapeutic services.

The employment potential for physical therapists is very good. An increasing number of rehabilitative services are being offered to people in need of relief from pain, improved range of motion, and orthopedic services. Available now, or just around the corner, are such new and exciting improvements as computerized services which may revolutionize some of the treatments being offered at this time.

Therapists in private practice are usually very successful. There are opportunities for full- and part-time work in physical therapy.

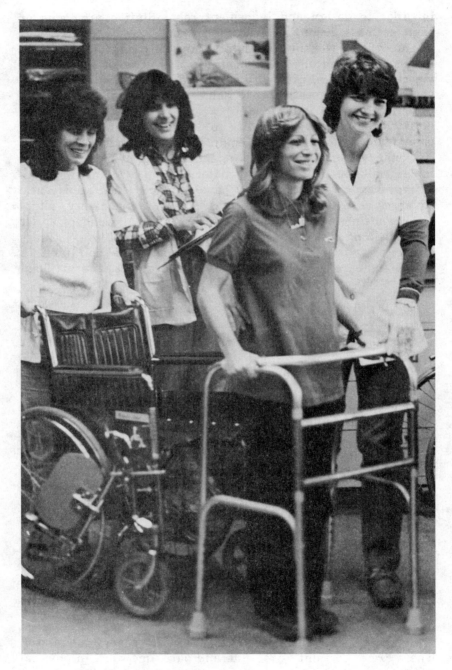

Many hours of physical therapy may be needed before standing is possible. (Photo by Marlene Wiener)

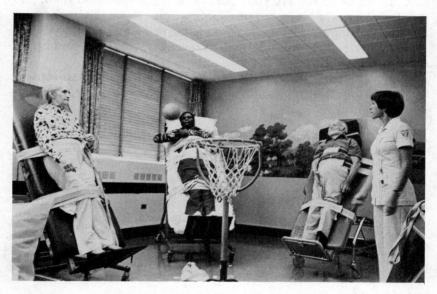

Playing basketball from tilt-tables is a post-operative activity used to develop arm musculature. (Photo courtesy of the American Physical Therapy Association)

Education and Advancement

In order to become a physical therapist, you must have a B.A. degree either in physical therapy or in a related field, such as physical education or health science, and completion of an additional certificate program in physical therapy. There is also the option of working for a master's degree in physical therapy. In addition, there are master's degree programs which offer advanced training for those already in the field.

All programs leading to the certificate in physical therapy must be accredited by the American Physical Therapy Association. In order to receive your license as a physical therapist, you must also pass a state board examination.

Career advancement depends on experience and advanced education, particularly for positions in teaching, research, and upper administrative levels.

Competition is likely to be the stiffest in large urban centers whereas opportunities should be good in suburban and rural areas of the country.

Employment Outlook

Beginning salaries in this field now range from $13,000 to $15,000 per year, depending on the location of the position. Average salaries for experienced therapists are about $18,000. Supervisors and therapists with advanced degrees earn over $25,000 in some areas.

Additional Information

Additional information about career opportunities in physical therapy may be secured by contacting:

The American Physical Therapy Association
1156 15th Street, NW
Washington, DC 20005

The National Association of Physical Therapists
7738 Mount Vernon
Lemon Grove, CA 92045

References

Arnheim, D., Auxter, D., and Crowe, W. *Principles and Methods of Adapted Physical Education and Recreation.* C.V. Mosby Co., 1977.

Breisky, W. *Physically Handicapped Children.* Doubleday, 1974.

Geddes, D. *Physical Activities for Individuals With Handicapping Conditions.* C.V. Mosby Co., 1974.

Occupational Therapy

Ask to Make Moccasins

The day of the big bazaar is at hand and you are very excited. For months, all of the men and women in the occupational therapy program have been working on items to sell today. They have decorated the old ward room to look like a summer carnival with booths along the walls housing games and wheels of fortune. There is a hot dog stand, a soda fountain, an old popcorn machine, and even a rented cotton candy machine. Staff members have donated records to play on the old record player, and one of your students is busily selling chances on the lovely handmade quilt that she and four other ladies have worked on throughout the year.

The weather has been hot and muggy all week. Everyone in the program has been afraid that it would rain and people would stay home. But the day is bright and sunny with a balmy August breeze that just might influence prospective customers to stay away from the beaches and come to the annual craft bazaar at the institution.

This is one of the few times that the residents at this large old state facility for the mentally ill have a chance to host an activity for friends, relatives, staff, and some of the curious and friendly neighbors who live in the community where the institution is located. It is a yearly event and one that is eagerly awaited by all of the staff and residents.

Since starting work here four months ago, you have been hearing about former bazaars held when the institution housed a great many other residents. The total population is now half of what it used to be. The remaining residents are less able to participate in some of the off-grounds activities that are scheduled by local churches and organizations that wish to provide opportunities for social interaction of clients with the outside community. You hope that this bazaar, the very first that you have planned, will not be a disappointment to everyone.

Eight large tables in the center of the room are arranged in a circle and brightly decorated with streamers. Each table displays a different craft shop, and, even now, some of your clients are still marking price tags as the first of the day's visitors enters the room.

In the center of the circle formed by the tables, you survey the items each of your craft shops is hoping to sell. As the only occupational therapist on staff, you have planned and guided the making of nearly every item for sale. The client selling chances on the quilt has been living here for many years and is fully capable of running the program in the sewing shop by herself. Her display of lacy pillows, Raggedy Ann dolls, ruffled aprons, and baby clothes has earned her a steady supply of customers who return every year.

Next to the sewing table are the small wooden toys, trays, cutting boards, and knickknack shelves that the men and women in the woodshop have made. This is the favorite activity of the men who live in the institution. Many clients seem to love the smooth feel of the wood and the soothing motions involved with sanding and finishing. It is also very satisfying to see the end result and know that it will grace someone's home or some child's room.

The ceramic shop clients have arranged their profusion of vases, pots, mugs, and free-form objects on a bright red cloth. Both the highly glazed items and the unglazed earthenware pots look very professional and artistic. This is your favorite activity and one that you intend to expand as soon as the new kiln arrives.

The fine art table is next and you smile as you observe the range of talent exhibited here. Some of the oil paintings and watercolors on display seem worthy of much more recognition. than the artists will get in this small show. But others reveal the true purpose of the activity, that of self-expression. Some of them look as angry or as unhappy as the artist who painted them. They may not reveal great talent but they certainly stir up the feelings of anyone who has the perception to see what is truly stated in them.

The mosaic and tile shop has the next table and you feel sure that the chessboards and colorful hot plates will sell well. Mosaic tilework is another favorite of the clients here at the institution. The repetitive activity is extremely soothing to people who are emotionally disturbed, and it is a good motor activity for people who are a bit physically stiff.

The photography and print shops have combined their tables with very pretty results. All summer, the clients in the print shop have been working on batik prints. They have matted some of the sensitive pictures taken by the people in the photography shop with the colorful batik prints. The creative idea was suggested by your assistant who has already had advance orders from people who have sent negatives of favorite pictures to be blown up and matted in the same way.

The last table contains the leatherwork. When you first arrived at the institution you were amazed at the high quality of the handtooled belts and purses made by the clients. You also admired the laced and beaded Indian items they made. At one point that first morning, you sat down next to one of the older ladies working on a yellow wallet. Introducing yourself only by your first name, you did not realize that the client thought you were a peer until, winking broadly, she picked up a piece of leather and handed it to you.

"Ask to make moccasins," she whispered. "When you ask to make moccasins they think you're ready to walk out of here."

Well, you haven't made any moccasins yet, and, judging by the brisk sales already being made by the small crowd gathering around the tables, your bazaar will be a success. The tension in your back is easing and you feel very proud of all the hard work your clients have accomplished. You're also feeling pretty proud of yourself, since you are often judged by this type of program.

What Do Occupational Therapists Do?

The field of occupational therapy is one of the brightest in the range of human service professions at the present time. Federal and state laws often mandate rehabilitation programs for the mentally ill, handicapped children, the aged, and armed forces veterans. This field has been growing as a result of public realization that good physical and psychological therapy programs were not helpful enough to restore many disabled people to a useful place in society.

The occupational therapist is trained to use and teach specific, purposeful activities to help a disabled person achieve or be restored to a vocational, social, personal, or recreational skill level that enables him to make as full use of his abilities as possible.

If you think you would be interested in a career as an occupational therapist, it would be a good idea for you to visit several of the places employing occupational therapists to see the wide variety of duties you might have.

Where the Jobs Are

Therapists work in hospitals, schools, nursing homes, sheltered workshops, the armed forces, private practice, and in many private and public agencies. Your responsibilities will vary depending on where you are working.

As an occupational therapist, you will often be part of a treatment team that may include any and all of the other human service professionals, as well as physicians and psychiatrists. You must be able to create a program for each patient that meets his individual needs.

The occupational therapist assists a teacher in developing instructional goals for fine motor development. (Photo by Marlene Wiener)

For example, you may be assessing, planning programs for, and evaluating a vocational workshop for retarded adults that will enable them to train for and eventually get jobs in actual work situations.

Or you may be working privately with a man who has suffered a crippling accident and must learn to perform self-care activities and specific skills that will prepare him for a career although confined to a wheelchair.

You might even be working with a group of mentally troubled adolescents who need to learn social skills and independence through recreational and educational activities like handicrafts or drama.

Your success as an occupational therapist will be measured by whether or not your patients are able to enter or reenter the community as responsible and contributing members. This is a job that demands a high level of energy, creativity, and adaptability.

Education

An occupational therapist must have completed a B.A. degree program and have six to ten months of supervised fieldwork. This qualifies you for the registered occupational therapist title. If you already have a B.A. in another area, you may apply for an entry-level master's program which requires about 45 credits in the field, in addition to a course of supervised fieldwork.

A certified occupational therapist assistant (C.O.T.A.) is a high school graduate or equivalent who has completed an approved one- or two-year certificate program from an accredited community or junior college. Occupational therapy assistants work under the direction of an occupational therapist.

In order to be professionally qualified you must pass an examination administered by the American Occupational Therapy Association.

There are not very many Ph.D. programs in this field but the number of universities offering them is growing.

Employment Outlook

Salary ranges for certified occupational therapists vary greatly depending on geographical location, but in general beginning therapists average about $13,000 per year. Therapists with more than five years of experience can expect to earn about $20,000 to $23,000 while therapists in administrative positions often earn as much as $30,000 yearly.

Additional Information

For additional information about career opportunities in occupational therapy contact:

American Occupational Therapy Association
6000 Executive Boulevard
Suite 200
Rockville, MD 20852

References

Copeland, M., Ford, L., and Solon, N. *Occupational Therapy For Mentally Retarded Children*. University Park Press, 1976.

Fidler, G.W., and Fidler, J.S. *Occupational Therapy*. Macmillan Publishing Company, 1963.

Mosey, A.C. *Activities Therapy*. Raven Press, 1973.

The Expressive Therapies: Music, Art, and Dance Therapy

Play A Simple Melody

You walk quickly up to the door of the low brick building, holding the umbrella in front of you to protect the armful of musical instruments you are bringing back. For the last month you have spent most of your evenings adapting bells, drumsticks, and picks so that the multiply handicapped children at the developmental center can make music. Today you are planning to try them out.

You also have brought a specially adapted Autoharp filled with differently shaped buttons to use with Maria, a blind little girl too retarded to learn Braille. You are hoping she can be taught to distinguish the shapes of the buttons so that she will learn to control what she plays.

"Hi Esther," you say breezily to the school secretary typing at her desk in the front office. "Wait until you hear the music we're going to make today!"

"Oh no," groans Esther, "and I was hoping to get some work done today."

"You just don't appreciate all the talent we have here," you call over your shoulder as you walk to your tiny office.

Since you only come to the center two days a week, you really don't rate an office of your own but the director took one look at all of the instruments, books, record players, chord organs, and tools that needed a secure place and offered you a supply closet large enough for several shelves, a desk, and a bookcase.

After dumping your equipment on the desk and hanging up your old blue raincoat, you check your plans for the day.

You have three groups this morning, one of them with Maria's class. Your eagerness to try out the adapted Autoharp amuses you because Maria learns so very slowly. It may be weeks before she realizes that differently shaped keys play different notes.

Nearly half of the children at this center are nonambulatory and many have difficulty with motor coordination so that it is hard to get sounds out of the usual instruments available for rhythm bands and music classes. A lot of the ones you use, therefore, have to be adapted to meet the needs of children who have only a slight amount of arm or hand pressure, or who have weak fingers or poor grasping skills. Some of the instruments are foot-operated like your clarina which has a mouthpiece connected to the instrument with flexible white plastic tubing. The clarina is placed on a nonskid surface and is played with the toes. A stand holds the mouthpiece in position.

Your favorite instrument for profoundly retarded children with some hand skills is the kalimba. Dulcet-toned, it consists of a number of metal keys mounted on a box resonator which produces a harmony of accordant sounds when the keys are barely touched. Children love the sounds and are delighted to make them.

As you place the instruments you are using today on the wheeled cart you use as you go from room to room, you make sure that there will be something suitable for each child, regardless of his handicap. You also review in your mind the emotional and physical needs of the children. Despite Esther's good-natured complaint about banging, you include the drums and sticks that allow children like Larry to bang away their frustrations and aggressions in a constructive and self-satisfying way.

Many severely retarded children have self-abusive behaviors. They may bang their heads against the wall or the floor or may slap, pick, and gouge at themselves until they bleed. Sometimes a good behavior modification program can control or redirect the behavior into more constructive channels, but sometimes nothing seems to work.

Larry is one of the head bangers. He is 15 years old and his head is very misshapen because the years of self-punishment have thickened the bone in his forehead. But sometimes, when he is in the midst of a cycle of abuse, you can get him to take a drum and a baton. He will bang away at that, obviously enjoying the percussive feelings he engenders. It is one of the joys of your job to watch his face light up when he sees you come into the room.

On Mondays and Wednesdays you work at the state institution which is a few miles outside of town. Some of the clients you work with are very similar in ability and behavior to the children here at the developmental center. They seem to have many more stereotypic behaviors than children who live at home. This is often attributed to the lack of environmental stimulation available at the institution.

Cultural and social deprivation used to be nearly total in the severely retarded institutionalized client. If a client was not able to at least sit up in a wheelchair, he would be condemned to a life in bed. His whole world would be contained in what he could see from a prone position. People would come into and move out of his line of vision and he would have no notion of why they were there, or even of the fact that they had an existence of their own. His days would be an endless round of sleeping, being fed, and being changed. An occasional toy might be waved in his face.

Your institution has changed a lot in the last three years, you reflect. The improvement is especially noticeable with this low functioning population. Now the clients are dressed in age-appropriate clothing and are placed in stretcher chairs or on mats for part of the day. They are brought outside in nice weather to feel the sun and the soft breezes of summer and are stimulated by recreation programs and by physical, speech, and music therapists. If still children, they participate in an education program. They are encouraged to feel textures, hear sounds and voices, see bright colors, rhythmic movements and movies, and to smell and taste a wide variety of scents and foods. They are repositioned frequently to stave off scoliosis or other physical problems associated with being bedridden.

You are part of the new program which is now shaping the institution and have been trained to see and to build on the nearly infinitesimal progress in each child's ability.

Firmly committed to a belief in the humanity of all people, you feel a great sense of achievement in the smiles and tiny strivings of these terribly handicapped people. You are rewarded in the knowledge that you enrich their world enough to sometimes cause them to try new movements or new sounds, and thus, to make the first moves towards self-expression.

On Fridays, as a total change of pace, you work in a church-sponsored Golden Age Club where you have a chance to display your musical talent as well as to utilize your years of psychological training. Some Fridays you organize square dancing, holiday song fests, or just a concert of nearly forgotten old favorites that bring back happy memories of youthful days, friends, and relatives long gone. But on other Fridays you help arthritic and stroke-affected people to make their own music. Once a month you meet with the church's social worker to discuss client responses to your program and to plan further activities. You may suggest that the social worker contact the client's family regarding important changes in behavior that may signal the need for medical attention.

Your life as a music therapist is busy and challenging, offering a great deal of opportunity for many varied activities with different groups of people.

What Is Expressive Therapy?

The use of art, music, and dance as therapy is probably as old as sentient man. Prehistoric cave drawings in Spain attest to the importance of capturing the ritual of the hunt in pictorial form. Paintings and murals from early Crete depict young boys and girls leaping over bulls in complicated dances. Many ancient records, including the Bible, mention the use of music and dance to calm and soothe or, conversely, to arouse or excite the spirit.

Throughout history these nonverbal expressions of creativity have affected the moods and documented the interests of non-literate peoples as they demonstrate their feelings of joy, hope, fear, sorrow, and anger through symbolic drawings, dances, and the making of music.

We are all aware of the power of music and art to stimulate feelings. Play a marching theme and we can immediately sense the atmosphere of flags flying, soldiers marching, and the lifting of spirit that is characteristic of patriotic music. Switch to a torchy love song and our mood changes to evoke the erotic feelings and memories we all carry within us.

But the therapeutic value of these expressive therapies is not gained so much by being a passive listener or observer. The therapy occurs when the discipline is used as a method of communication by the client.

Normal, healthy people can benefit from participation in expressive therapy programs in that they are encouraged to act out their feelings in creative ways rather than to internalize them or to express them in negative ways. Adolescents, particularly, benefit from activities that provide acceptable outlets for their mercurial emotions.

Handicapped children and adults have had, until recently, less access to music, art, dance, and other forms of creative expression for a number of reasons:

1. Special educators and other professionals who work with the disabled spend years in training. Since music and art are also very demanding fields to pursue, there are still few people with dual proficiencies.

2. Severely handicapped people who are in residential placements usually are cared for by nonspecialist staffs. Economic reasons made the hiring of experts in artistic fields very unlikely until recently.

3. There are many practical difficulties which must be over-
    come before the severely handicapped person can express
    his feelings by creating his own art, music, or dance.

In order to work with the mentally or emotionally disturbed
person, a therapist must be trained in psychology. Art, particularly, may be viewed by treatment teams as an integral part of a
person's therapy. It serves as a nonverbal outlet for a person's
fantasies or feelings which can be studied by the treatment team
in order to gain a better understanding of the client and his
personality.

Music and dance may also be utilized for the same purpose. In
the case of dance, the therapist works to change or heighten a
person's body awareness and to encourage him to express formerly unconscious feelings and emotions through improvised
movement. Often, too, the therapist will imitate or mirror the
client's actions in order to provide him with visual feedback
about his posture, breathing patterns, and general emotional
appearance.

Music is used as both passive and active therapy for the
mentally ill. As previously mentioned, music can be used to
create specific moods or to calm an agitated person. It also
serves as an outlet for self-expression.

The physically handicapped person may find it very difficult
to utilize art tools and musical instruments without having them
adapted for his particular skills. The expressive therapist must
be able to adapt or to find adapted equipment.

The areas generally covered by the expressive therapies have
grown out of the experiences of teachers, musicians, and artists
who have observed that the medical, social, and psychological
benefits of the programs far outweigh the artistic value.

It is not at all necessary for the person in therapy to have any
knowledge or talent in the creative area used for expression.
Success in painting a picture, playing a melody, or creating an
interlude of dancing often leads directly to increased self-esteem
and greater social integration because the clients become more
aware of their ability to have an impact upon their environment.

Therapists who work with retarded or otherwise severely
handicapped children know how normal children respond at re-
spective stages in their physical and mental development and are
able to compare data with the developmental stages achieved by
the handicapped child in order to devise programs which encourage progress.

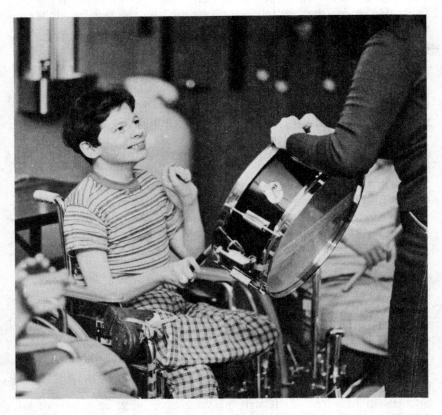

Music therapy aids in developing listening skills as well as gross and fine motor coordination. (Photo by Marlene Wiener, courtesy of Woodbridge State School)

Where Do Expressive Therapists Work?

Expressive therapists play a valuable role in helping individuals or groups adjust to new life situations such as placement in nursing homes or hospitalization after accidents, strokes, or other disabling diseases. They are often found on treatment teams of hospitals and residential schools. They are employed by community mental health centers, day-care centers, geriatric centers, large urban churches, and many private or public human service agencies with budgets that permit social enrichment and therapy programs.

Music, art, and dance therapists are also being utilized more often in correctional facilities for both juveniles and adults. The expense of including what may appear to be a "budgetary frill" is outweighed by the improvement in morale and concurrent reduction of disciplinary problems that often seem to occur when the facility provides creative outlets for the expression of feelings.

In private practice, music, art, and dance therapists may work with individuals or groups. They may work directly with clients or train other personnel to carry out the techniques involved in a creative therapy program.

Many therapists are involved in research in both hospitals and universities and frequently serve as consultants to schools, institutions, and hospice programs for the terminally ill. Public recreation programs may also employ an expressive therapist as a part-time consultant to train paraprofessionals and volunteers, or for carrying out direct therapeutic services to individuals or to groups of clients.

Some therapists are employed in administrative positions as program directors or supervisors in institutions, schools, and hospitals. Others are involved with teaching in colleges and universities.

This is a rapidly growing field with much room for further research and increasingly varied employment opportunities. Within the mental health field, the expressive therapies are growing in status and acceptance. Professional standards and criteria for training are still in the process of development. For this reason, there is a feeling of excitement and anticipation in many of the people who work in this field.

Even in these current years of economic recession, opportunities in this field are good for the person who is willing to devote the time, effort, and money necessary for training.

How to Become a Music Therapist

A person who wishes to become a music therapist must first graduate from a four-year college with a bachelor's degree in music. At least half of all earned college credits must be in courses such as music theory, arranging, music conducting, history of music, instrumental and sometimes vocal courses, as well as courses in music therapy. The college must be approved by the National Association for Music Therapy (N.A.M.T.) or the American Association for Music Therapy (A.A.M.T.). Many college or university catalogues will indicate approval by these organizations. A list of approved colleges and universities can be obtained by writing directly to these associations. (See page 94 for addresses.)

In addition to coursework in music, a student intending to become a therapist must study psychology, sociology, education, and biology.

A six-month clinical internship or practicum must also be completed either during college or after graduation from an accredited college. All internship programs first must be approved by the professional associations for music therapy. Programs are usually found with developmental centers, schools, community mental health centers, or other locations where an employed professional music therapist can supervise.

A number of accredited institutions now offer graduate degrees in music therapy. Here, someone with a bachelor's degree in music may get additional training in specific areas of music therapy and gain experience and further knowledge of the different types of people who benefit from music therapy programs.

Since this is a relatively new area, it is still possible to hold a supervisory or administrative position in the field without a graduate degree, but future job advancement will most probably be predicated on higher-level degrees as well as experience. There are only a few doctoral level programs offered at the present time, but it is expected that a degree at this level will be necessary in the near future for therapists who wish to teach at the college or university level as well as for those seeking top administrative positions.

Certification

In order to attain the title of professional music therapist you must be registered by the National Association for Music

Therapy. You will then be a registered music therapist (R.M.T.). The American Association of Music Therapy grants a Certificate of Music Therapy (C.M.T.). These two organizations are responsible for establishing and monitoring the criteria for music therapy programs of study. At the present time there are no state or government agencies offering certification or licenses in this area although some states have civil service titles for music therapists.

The American Association of Music Therapists has recently upgraded their criteria and now awards the Certificate of Music Therapy only at the master's level.

Music therapists who work in public schools must generally possess state certification as a teacher of elementary, secondary, or special education.

Employment Outlook

Salaries in this field vary greatly depending upon the state in which you are working. In general, entry-level salaries are commensurate with the starting salaries of certified teachers in the state. For experienced therapists and those who are in supervisory positions, salaries may be as high as $25,000. Music therapists who are in private practice set their own fee schedules, usually at an hourly rate.

Becoming an Art Therapist

Graduate level training is generally considered to be necessary for a position in the field of art therapy. Training programs in this area are still being modified and expanded but the American Art Therapy Association (A.A.T.A.) has assumed the responsibility for establishing the criteria for registration as a professional art therapist.

In order to prepare for a career in art therapy, you must have graduated from an accredited college or university with a major concentration in fine arts as well as with coursework in the social and behavioral sciences. It is also beneficial to gain experience as a volunteer or part-time employee in an agency or school which serves special needs populations.

You must have a firm grounding in all of the techniques and theory necessary to achieve proficiency in art and the teaching of art. Then you must add training and experience in psychology, sociology, or special education. This will enable you to use the medium in a therapeutic manner.

Once you have graduated from college, you are then required to enter a master's degree program in art therapy in order to become a registered art therapist. Most graduate schools require at least two years of coursework as well as a program of supervised fieldwork. This fieldwork, or internship, is generally for a minimum of 600 hours and takes place in a facility utilizing creative expression where there is a registered art therapist on staff who will be able to supervise your work. During this period, you will be able to refine your art therapy technique. You will also be encouraged to enter into an art therapy program. This is an effective way to gain insights into the therapy experience and into your own motivations and feelings. Upon completion of the graduate school program, you will receive a master's degree. The title conferred depends upon the institution from which you are graduating and may range from Master of Science in Art Education to Master of Creative Arts in Therapy.

Additional training is available in order to acquire greater proficiency in specialized areas within the field. You may be able to focus attention on the development of techniques for working with autistic or emotionally disturbed children, the physically handicapped, socially maladjusted or culturally deprived children, geriatric clients, and many more.

Certification

There is no specific certification or license necessary in order to become an art therapist but registration with the American Art Therapy Association will establish you as having attained a minimum level of training in the field.

As with music therapists, public schools may require you to have an appropriate educational certificate before they will employ you. Also, some state or other governmental facilities may require you to take a civil service examination.

Employment Outlook

Salaries in the field of art therapy depend upon the quality of experience and the geographic location of the position. Starting salaries for therapists with an M.A. degree may range from $10,000 to $17,000 per year. Experienced art therapists may earn up to $30,000 if they are in administrative positions. Therapists in private practice charge an average of $35.00 per hour.

How to Become a Dance Therapist

Dance therapy, as a profession, is still in the process of establishing the criteria necessary for setting uniform standards in the field. The American Dance Therapy Association (A.D.T.A.) is charged with this responsibility and, as of 1983, requires a master's degree in dance therapy in order to be recognized as a professional dance therapist.

There are also a number of nonacademic training programs available in hospitals and agencies where specialized courses in dance therapy techniques are offered to staff members who work with geriatric, autistic, or mentally ill clients.

If you are interested in a career as a dance therapist, your undergraduate college program should include the study of dance as well as a liberal arts education emphasizing the behavioral and social sciences. Coursework in physiology, biology, and anatomy are also important to the dance therapist. These will give you an understanding of the physical aspects of body movement as well as the kinds of handicaps which necessitate adaptations to therapy programs.

Graduate education for dance therapy, as for the other expressive therapies, consists of two years of full-time study as well as a supervised internship which is usually undertaken during the last six months of the program.

A master's degree in dance therapy is awarded after you have completed all of the school requirements. At the present time, there are no doctoral level programs in dance therapy, but, as with the other expressive therapies, this degree will become necessary to meet the needs of the profession as it develops.

Certification

The only certification available in this field at present is provided by the American Dance Therapy Association which requires a minimum of master's level training before you can be accepted for registration as a member of the organization.

Employment Outlook

Beginning yearly salaries for registered dance therapists range from $10,000 to $17,000 depending upon your experience and education in the field. Some states have classified the dance therapist as a civil service title.

Dance therapists who have set up private practices or who offer consultant services usually establish hourly rates which may range from $15.00 to $50.00, again depending on the expertise of the therapist and the service being rendered.

Additional Information

For additional information about the expressive therapies write to:

National Association for Music Therapy, Inc.
P. O. Box 610
Lawrence, KS 66044

American Association for Music Therapists
Department of Music and Music Education
777 Education Building, New York University
Washington Square
New York, NY 10003

American Art Therapy Association
Two Skyline Place
5203 Leesburg Pike
Falls Church, VA 22041

National Committee on Arts for the Handicapped
1701 K Street, NW
Suite 801
Washington, DC 20006

American Dance Therapy Association
2000 Century Plaza
Suite 230
Columbia, MD 21044

American Alliance for Health, Physical Education,
  and Recreation
1201 16th Street, NW
Washington, DC 20006

National Institute for Mental Health
Division of Information
5600 Fishers Lane
Rockville, MD 20853

References

Amary, I. *Creative Recreation For the Mentally Retarded.* Charles C. Thomas, 1975.

Arnheim, D., Auxter, D., and Crowe, W. *Principles and Methods of Adapted Physical Education and Recreation.* C.V. Mosby Co., 1977.

Bailey, Philip. *They Can Make Music.* Oxford University Press, 1973.

Caskey, Alan. *The Recreation Center Operation Manual.* A.S. Barnes and Co., Inc., 1972.

Clark, C., and Chadwick, D. *Clinically Adapted Instruments for the Multiply Handicapped.* Magnamusic-Baton, 1980.

Krone, A. *Art Instruction for Handicapped Children.* Love Publishing Co., 1978.

Naumburg, M. *Dynamically Oriented Art Therapy: Its Principles and Practices.* Grune and Stratton, 1966.

Reichard, C., and Blackburn, D. *Music Based Instruction for the Exceptional Child.* Love Publishing Co., 1973.

Schmolling, P., Burger, W., and Youkeles, M. *Helping People: A Guide to Careers in Mental Health.* Prentice-Hall, Inc., 1981.

Szymanski, L., and Tanguay, P. (Eds.). *Emotional Disorders of Mentally Retarded Persons.* University Park Press, 1980.

4. PARAPROFESSIONALS

A paraprofessional is a person who has not had education in his designated field of employment beyond the bachelor's degree. Quite often, his educational qualifications are considerably less. Nevertheless, the duties assigned to paraprofessionals are often very demanding and are sometimes similar to or even the same as those of some professionals. The paraprofessional, however, works under the direction of the professional.

In this section, the social service paraprofessional is discussed. It is a career area that is becoming one of the most important within the human services. There are many jobs in this field that are filled by aides because of their cost effectiveness as well as their demonstrated ability.

Many of the government funding programs available for staffing social service programs are for paraprofessional job titles because more personnel can be hired for the same money than if the salaries were being paid to professionals.

Another important reason why paraprofessional jobs are important career areas in this field is because these positions can be filled by people who are in need of employment and have few marketable skills. Within the network of human services, paraprofessionals can receive their training on an in-service basis, gain experience on the job, and then move on to more lucrative jobs in the business world.

Human Service Aide

Four Viewpoints

The restaurant is crowded and noisy with people rushing through their lunches in hopes of getting in a little Christmas shopping on the way back to work. The walls and light fixtures are festooned with tinsel and bells, and a large, decorated silver tree in the middle of the room makes it hard to see if your three friends have arrived before you. But, off in a corner, you see Bill waving to you.

"I guess we're the first ones," you observe, as you take off your coat and hang it on the back of your chair. "When do you have to be back to work?"

"Not until one thirty," he answers. "I told my boss that this was sort of a class reunion and he said I could have an extra half hour."

"You're lucky. I have to be back in the office by one," you sigh. "I'll be interviewing clients all afternoon. We're so backed up these days that we're all carrying nearly double our usual caseload."

"What exactly do you do at the county welfare department?" asks Bill. "You're the only one from our class that got a job over there."

"I'm an income maintenance worker," you state rather proudly.

"That sounds pretty important."

"Well, it makes me feel important. I don't make very much money and I've only been there six months but I've helped a lot of people and I've learned a lot about people, too.

"For the most part," you continue, "I interview applicants to see if they are eligible for assistance. Sometimes I have to do a document check on them and once or twice I've been sent to do a home visit. Actually, the income maintenance supervisor does the home visits most of the time," you admit.

"I've been doing some home visits lately, too," Bill interjects. "The agency I work for maintains a Senior Citizen's Center and I'm what they call an outreach worker."

"What does that mean?" you ask with interest.

"Well, I canvass some of the neighborhoods in town to tell families about the Center and to find out whether there are elderly people who have problems we can help them to solve. We want the Center to be able to serve the people who are too frail or too poor to be able to get to the Center for programs. For instance, we can send hot meals, once a day, to someone's home." Bill's eyes sparkle with enthusiasm as he talks, "Also, if some elderly people aren't able to get around to stores, we're organizing a group of volunteers who will spend a couple of hours a week buying groceries or going to department stores to shop for clients. We also have a van that takes people to doctor's appointments or to parties at the center.

"What we're trying to do," he continues, "is to make it possible for older people to live in their own homes as long as they can. It's cheaper for the taxpayers, and the clients are certainly a lot happier at their own homes than in some dreary nursing home."

"That really sounds interesting," you comment, "but I thought Judy told me you were involved with getting kids inoculated for school."

"I was doing that during the summer," Bill explains. "One of the great things about working for a small agency is that you get to be involved with different projects. They put you wherever you're needed most. You never get bored."

"What do you think is keeping Judy and Mary Anne?" you ask worriedly. "I don't have very much time and I really wanted to see them."

Gazing toward the door, Bill smiles broadly and waves a greeting to the two young women hurrying toward the table. "Here they are now," he observes.

"I got lost trying to find Judy's group home," confesses Mary Anne breathlessly. "I drove right by it twice! I guess I expected to see a big sign saying GROUP HOME or something."

"Group homes are supposed to be indistinguishable from any other home." Judy explains, "The whole purpose of moving people out of institutions and into group homes is to help them live normal, quiet, uneventful lives just like everyone else."

"Well, you certainly will accomplish the uneventful part," laughs Mary Anne. "You don't even have a name on the mailbox. No one will ever be able to find any of you!"

"We haven't had time for that," Judy returns. "We've only been there for two weeks. We just hung the living room curtains this morning. The guys have been wonderful! They're adjusting a lot faster than we thought they would considering they've lived most of their lives in institutions. All six of our clients are retarded, but they're not children. They are all over 20 now."

"But I thought you told me that they were going to school," Bill says.

"Not school," explains Judy, "they have jobs at the workshop. Frances, Tom, and Betty are in the contract program. They make ball point pens. Actually, they assemble the pens. Someone else makes the parts. Alan, Willy, and John are in the crafts program. They work with an occupational therapist in a woodworking shop."

"Do they get paid by the hour?" asks Mary Anne.

"The contract program pays a piece rate," answers Judy. "The workshop pays by the hour but it's a special wage scale based on government regulations.

"They started going to the workshop while they were still in the institution so they didn't have to adjust to that when they moved into the home. They've all had to learn a lot of new things in the last two weeks," she continues. "They've been to the supermarket to shop, they do their own housework, and they're learning to plan what they want to do in their spare time. One of the things they're finding very difficult is to do things individually, instead of all together."

"Your job really sounds interesting," observes Bill. "It's like being a house mother."

"A little. But I really feel more like a friend than a mother," observes Judy sincerely. "Jim, the other counselor, and I really try to get group decisions on how the home should operate."

"How do you know what to do?" asks Bill. "None of the courses we took last year taught you how to work in a group home."

"Oh, we have in-service training programs all the time. During the day, while the others are at work, Jim and I are still learning to handle the problems that come up constantly. The association that runs the home gives us as much help as they can. We have consultations with the social workers and the psychologist, and they monitor us pretty carefully right now. As time goes by, if there aren't any big problems, we'll be more on our own," Judy finishes. "It's really very challenging, and a lot of fun too."

Mary Anne picks up her menu and looks at it for a moment before putting it down. "I have something to tell you all," she says excitedly, "I found a job!"

"I thought so," observes Judy. "You've been bursting with something ever since I got into your car."

"What kind of a job?" you ask.

"Well," says Mary Anne, savoring every word, "I went back to the employment service at college, to see if they had anything open yet, and Mrs. Baines sent me over to the recreation center in Bakerville. They have a new program of day care for handicapped preschool children . . . so that their mothers can go back to work."

"And you're going to work over there?" Bill inquires.

"Yes, I am," answers Mary Anne. "I had an interview yesterday for an aide's position, and my 60 hours of human service courses at the college, along with all that baby-sitting I did while I was in high school, made them decide to give me a job. But the best part of it all," she continues, "is that they will set my hours so that I can go back and get a teaching degree in early childhood education for the handicapped. That's a good field to go into these days."

"That's just great, Mary Anne," you declare. "This can be a real celebration now that we're all working. Shall we splurge and order the special of the day?"

Paraprofessionals in Human Service Positions

During the past two decades, a new career level has emerged as the result of a steadily increasing need for entry-level workers who have technical knowledge of professional skill areas.

The people who work in these jobs are called paraprofessionals because, although they do not have the credentials or the certifications to qualify for professional occupations, they have fulfilled a program of study, generally 60 hours or more at the college level, in a particular field.

Paraprofessionals are now making important contributions to the fields of law, medicine, education, nursing, science, and industry. Today there are very few professional areas that do not utilize paraprofessionals to some degree.

Within the field of human services, social or human service aides perform many valuable and necessary roles. Their competence and cost effectiveness have led government and private agencies to employ them in many different capacities. They constitute an economic means of helping to meet the constantly growing and changing human service needs of today's world.

Social service aides can be found in positions that supplement the work of professional social workers, rehabilitation and recreation counselors, and occupational therapists. They always work under the supervision of the professional staff.

Often, the human service aide serves as the first contact made by clients seeking help of one kind or another. They may set up the initial meeting, explain the services of the agency, assist clients with forms and paperwork, and take care of minor problems like change of address forms. They generally take care of a large part of the filing and recordkeeping. Although routine paperwork is an important part of the job, the most essential aspect is the direct interaction with clients.

Nature of the Work

Social service aides work in a variety of settings and perform a wide range of tasks. From agency to agency they may also have a number of different job titles, most of which overlap to some degree.

Income maintenance workers and *income maintenance specialists* do the intake work involved in determining an applicant's eligibility for income assistance.

Casework aides or *assistants* work directly with clients under the supervision of social workers. They may refer families in crisis to counseling services, assist families in obtaining adequate housing, food stamps, or medical care, and help them to apply for unemployment or Social Security benefits. Casework aides sometimes take clients to medical clinics or health centers in order to insure that they carry out needed tests or treatment programs. They may also be used to assist social workers with programs for juveniles who are in trouble with the law.

These aides may also spend a great deal of time on routine telephone duties such as gathering information about clients from themselves or from other agencies, or, conversely, assisting clients to cut through some of the red tape that surrounds most of the procedures for getting either direct hands-on or monetary aid.

Neighborhood or *outreach workers*, on the other hand, can usually be found outside of the office doing a lot of the legwork. They carry out assignments necessitating personal contact with the client or his family and neighbors. These aides research needs and refer any routine matters to counselors or to whichever community agency is best suited to help. If the individual or family has a more complicated problem, an aide will report this to a supervisor for resolution.

Essentially, neighborhood workers are assigned to certain parts of a community or certain neighborhoods within a city. They facilitate the flow of information and services between that area and the agency to directly benefit the members of the community. In addition, these workers may assist in conducting surveys, administering routine health programs, and also must prepare detailed reports of their activities to keep supervisors informed.

Employment aides assist clients to become more employable by referring them to training and vocational programs. They also provide job information and help clients to fill out applications. Once clients have secured jobs, employment aides may sometimes work with them to insure that they adjust to the specific demands of the job or to get additional training for upward mobility in their skill areas.

Homemaker or *health aides* spend time working directly in people's homes. They provide direct care or housekeeping assistance to clients who are ill or otherwise unable to keep up with the chores of maintaining an independent living situation. This may be because of chronic or accidental disability, emotional difficulties of a temporary nature, or because of a client's advanced age and helplessness.

Some of the other jobs you may have if you become a social service aide are: alcohol recovery unit counselor, transitional employment counselor, social work designate, social service technician, information coordinator, education aide, recreation worker, patient care coordinator, youth counselor, mental health technician, career counselor, vocation aide, residential supervisor, residence counselor, or client advocate.

Where Will You Be Working?

Most of the employment opportunities for social or human service aides are to be found in the inner-city areas of large metropolitan centers. Even small communities, however, usually have public and private agencies providing information and assistance to people who are in need.

Welfare agencies and departments, run by local governments or religious organizations, employ the vast majority of social or human service aides. Jobs are to be found in offices run by city, county, or state welfare departments, neighborhood centers, family and children's service agencies, halfway houses and group homes for people who have been hospitalized or institutionalized, sheltered workshops, and vocational or rehabilitation centers.

Other aides may work in schools, hospitals, clinics, public health service organizations, or public housing projects.

Employment opportunities in the entire career area are better than in all other human service professions at this time. There are also many opportunities for part-time work. This is a boon for college students who are working towards a degree but must work in order to support themselves and pay for college as they attend. It is also a useful arrangement for women with small children. Part-time employment makes it possible for women to spend more time at home when their children are young while still remaining a part of the working world.

The growing need to provide services to our aging population as well as the increased demand for programs for the very young disabled child are another factor in the expansion of jobs available for social service paraprofessionals.

Another factor related to the positive employment outlook for the social service worker is the current economic condition. There is a dramatic saving of taxpayer's money when aides are employed to perform services formerly part of the domain of the higher paid professional. There have been many studies to evaluate the efficacy of the paraprofessional as compared to the professional. Such studies have indicated that noncredentialed workers make important contributions to the quality and the delivery of services and achieve outcomes equal to those obtained by professionals when they are properly in-serviced and supervised.

Training, Advancement, and Employment Opportunities

Some social service aide positions do not require a high school diploma in order to enter at the clerical level but may be granted after successful completion of a proficiency examination. In government positions, this examination may be a formal civil service procedure. If the position is located in a private agency, the test may be quite informal. The amount of responsibility given to the position, however, usually depends upon the level of education or years of experience needed in order to attain the position.

Personal qualities such as a good ability to communicate and establish a sense of rapport with others will carry a lot of weight when you are being considered for a position. Also, previous work experience in similar employment situations, clerical and typing skills, or a knowledge of one of the foreign languages needed when working with ethnic populations will be very helpful when you are looking for a job.

Within the area of human services, an individual may also be hired because of a genuine need for work and good potential for success in the position. Many former clients are often hired as aides after being trained. In addition, many people are hired as part of government programs such as the Job Corps. These have proven to be sound ways of providing subsidized job opportunities to low income individuals as a method of assisting welfare populations to gain the working skills necessary to move out into the larger work force.

Although most advancement is achieved through a combination of on-the-job training, work experience, and further education, many community and state colleges offer two-year programs for social service aide or human service aide positions. The course of study usually includes sociology, psychology, and courses offering training in interviewing, observation, behavior modification, counseling, and community studies as well as field experience in local agencies. College graduates who have degrees in areas not related to social service also are hired as social service aides.

Starting salaries for full-time aides with no prior experience or formal education in the field average about $8000. Large metropolitan agencies usually pay a higher amount and smaller rural centers pay less. Government agencies usually pay more than private ones. Experienced aides may earn as much as $15,000.

Most positions are in offices and agencies and are generally 9 A.M. to 5 P.M., five days a week. However, some positions may require evening and weekend work as these are hours when clients can be reached.

Additional Information

Additional information may be obtained from city, county, or state departments of social service or welfare, and from all local offices of your state employment service. You may also wish to contact:

American Federation of State, County and Municipal Employees
1625 L Street, NW
Washington, DC 20036

Council for Standards in Human Service Education
Southern Regional Education Board
130 Sixth Street, NW
Atlanta, GA 30313

National Organization of Human Services
Box 999, Loretto Station
Denver, CO 80236

National Organization of Human Service Educators
Indiana University—Purdue University
2101 Coliseum Boulevard East
Fort Wayne, IN 46805

References

Dugger, J.G. *The New Professional: Introduction of the Human Services/Mental Health Worker.* Brooks/Cole Publishing Co., 1975.

Gartner, A. *Paraprofessionals and Their Performance: A Survey of Education, Health, and Social Service Programs.* Praeger Publishers, 1971.

Hawes, G.R. *Careers Tomorrow: Leading Growth Fields for College Graduates.* New American Library, 1979.

Janes, Avenson, and Harvey. "Paraprofessionals in Mental Health Delivery Services," *Journal of Mental Health Administration.* Vol. 8, No. 1, 1981.

Lehman, M., Bailey, B., and Cunningham, H.M. "C.E.T.A. Personnel as a Manpower Resource for Mental Health Agencies," *Journal of Mental Health Administration*, Vol. 8, No. 1, 1981.

Sobey, F. *The Nonprofessional Revolution in Mental Health.* Columbia University Press, 1970.

Splaver, S. *Paraprofessions: Careers of the Future and the Present.* Messner, 1972.

5. THE PRIVATE SECTOR

American Dreams

José is a nine-year-old Cuban boy whose family came to Florida two years ago in order to escape the present political situation in Cuba. José's father is a pharmacist by profession but his credentials are not acceptable in this country. He had to take two jobs in order to pay the rent on the small crowded apartment that is now home to José, his parents, and his three young sisters. During the daytime José's father works in a car wash and in the evenings he is a waiter in one of the large Spanish restaurants in Miami. He works long hours, has no benefits, and cannot yet afford to take the classes at night that will help him to qualify as a pharmacist in this country.

José's mother works at home, making children's clothing on the old and noisy sewing machine that was provided by the man who comes every Wednesday to pick up the clothing she has made and to bring her new dresses to sew. She is paid by the piece, at a rate much lower than she could make in a factory, but she is able to stay at home with her small children since there is no one else who can take care of them.

When José is not in school, he helps his mother by shopping for groceries or by helping to watch his little sisters. He also sings with the boys choir at the church. José's family does not own a car, a telephone, or a television set. But, on Saturdays, José and his father go fishing and his mother cooks the day's catch in a lovely soup. In the evening, José and his family eat the soup and sit outside the apartment with friends from Cuba. They talk of the old days in their village and often sing songs about home and the friends they have left behind.

On Sundays, José sings at all three masses. His family comes to the last one. José loves to look down from the loft and see his father in a black suit and his mother in a bright dress and high-heeled shoes. He is proud of his pretty little sisters in ruffled dresses and white socks. After church and their Sunday dinner, they all walk together, through the park, looking at the flowers and at the American children playing games. José longs to play ball games with the other children but he is not allowed. He is needed at home.

In school, José's favorite class is art. Here, he does not feel the need to learn English to succeed and he loves to draw and to paint. When his teacher looks at his pictures, she can often see in them the conflict of his strong love for his family and his yearning to be free to play with his peers. José loves strong, bright colors and bold lines. His teacher, who is also an art therapist, encourages him to express himself as fully as possible. José feels so good when he is making a picture. He paints his mother while she is sewing, the light from the ceiling bulb making her dark hair shine against the dingy white wall. He paints himself with eager eyes as he watches a baseball game through the open window in his kitchen. His arms rest on the broken windowsill and his three sisters play on the floor behind him. Once he drew a picture of his father standing in the doorway of his own drugstore in Cuba, back in the days when his father was an important man whose opinions were respected by everyone in the village. In the picture, José makes his father taller than all of the other men.

Over his own bed, José has taped his favorite picture. It is a large white fishing boat like the one he plans to own when he becomes rich. He will take all the wealthy Americans out to fish in the ocean. He has painted them standing at the railing with lines in the foamy water and big fish jumping up to grab the bait. Everyone is smiling and showing big white teeth because it is so good to be fishing on José's boat. The sky is full of greedy pelicans with their beaks full of fish and, at the wheel of the boat, José is wearing a bright yellow shirt and waving a loving good-bye to his mother who does not need to sew anymore now that José is so rich. . . .

Private Sources for Support

José, though poor in material goods and living in the heart of a minority neighborhood, is far from culturally deprived. His everyday world is rich with his ethnic heritage. He is active, bright, and fortunate enough to be the son of an educated father who has goals for the future. He also is part of an intact and loving family. His poverty is probably only temporary. His church provides him with social as well as spiritual guidance. And, in school, his art teacher is well-grounded as an art therapist. She is able to help José and the other children in his class to adjust to life in a new country by providing a way of expressing their fears and frustrations.

José and his family have a lot of things going for them. Their chances of doing well in the United States are good because of the positive nature of three strong social influences which are serving to support the family at this crucial time. The strength of the family itself is a major force helping the family to survive the uprooting. José's family is closely knit and has clearly defined goals. Although they are living in poverty at the present time, everyone old enough to understand is helping the family to become educated and respected in a country where they can be free to express their political views in safety.

The other two support systems working for José and his family are the church and the school. The church, as a private social service agency, and the school, as a branch of public tax-payer supported assistance, are giving the right amount of help and guidance to José. In this chapter, private services will be discussed in order to provide you with an understanding of the large part they play in the total scope of the human services.

José and his family are used to begin this section as an example of a case with a strong family support system. When the family does not meet the needs of its members, there is a reason to turn to other support agencies.

The family unit has continued to operate as one of the most effective human service agencies. When successful, it is small, private, and structured in such a way that it provides the optimum in health care, emotional nurturance, physical safety, social interaction, and education for its members. A good family normally contains at least one adult role model of each sex. It provides peers with whom to learn competition and cooperation. It offers constant opportunities to learn responsibility and the benefits of loyalty. It teaches the joys of sociability, the need for rules and organization, and the respect for the life and property of others. It provides tasks suitable to each developmental level and demonstrates the contributions of each generation. A good family provides all of this as well as the mantle of security that arises when people feel accepted and loved.

Fortunately, most families do a creditable job of preparing their members to meet the problems of the times in which they live. It is when they break down in some way, or run into a crisis they cannot overcome that they need some form of temporary help until they can function independently again. Usually, this help is as simple as the loan of money from a friend to enable them to meet an unexpected emergency or the services of a neighbor who comes in to cook and clean during a time when the mother is incapacitated. When friends and helpful neighbors are not available, a family must turn to more formal methods of assistance. It is here, at the very edge of family breakdown, that the private human service agencies do their greatest work. It is only when large numbers of people, whole groups of families, or statistically relevant populations are in need that the government is authorized by taxpayers to use funds and personnel to intervene.

Many private organizations function to offer assistance to families and individuals whose need is of an immediate and short-term nature. The Red Cross, for instance, is prepared to offer help ranging from clothing donations to loans when people are hit by disasters such as floods and hurricanes. Organized religious groups are also able to mobilize help during emergencies.

In José's case, his church provides many kinds of assistance to families whose needs range from finding housing and jobs in order to survive to protecting family members from culture shock. The church becomes a place where José's family can feel respected. Here the children can observe their parents move socially among peers who value their knowledge and company. The church also provides José and his sisters with positive social activities acceptable to their parents who are unfamiliar with the kinds of social interaction available in a new country. These activities help to give the children a sense of "belonging."

Religious groups have helped families weather all forms of problems. Originally, they were closest to the families geographically as well as spiritually and could offer assistance that was unique to the problems of each individual. Also, the people providing the help were friends, or at least acquaintances of the recipient. Today, many of the church-supported human service agencies are removed from the areas they are serving both culturally and geographically. The helpful neighbor has been replaced by a professional caseworker, homemaker, nurse, or other provider. In many cases the agencies are nationwide in scope.

Private organizations which exist in order to help immigrant families assimilate are often founded by groups of earlier immigrants who understand the problems unique to the population they intend to serve. They may utilize government funding sources but they build their programs around the specific needs of a certain group. They tend to cease functioning when these needs no longer exist. This is not always true of human service agencies. Many of them will redirect their services when the needs have been fulfilled.

Private agencies and service organizations help individuals and families survive problems such as alcoholism, drug addiction, and child and wife abuse. They teach how to care for retarded or seriously disabled children and how to live with crippling or otherwise debilitating diseases. There are private agencies which offer direct help, money, or the services of a caseworker who will help find assistance.

The third support system helping José in our illustration is one of the many public services available to all Americans—the public school system. José's city is only too aware of the problems of his family and of the many other Cuban families struggling to survive. The school is faced with educating a large number of Spanish-speaking children. They also must deal with the many other problems associated with large foreign populations, such as the truancy of children who are kept at home to care for younger siblings when a mother is forced to work outside of the home and the hostility of settled communities towards the newcomers. For José, his art teacher will have an enormous influence on his successful integration and may help him to determine a career selection later in life. Her skill as an art therapist assists him to find a rewarding and constructive outlet for the expression of his homesickness as well as his uncertainties about life in the United States. She also helps him to find a highly visible way to gain status in the eyes of his peers as well as his family.

Children of immigrant populations often attend schools run by the religious organizations to which they belong. These private schools serve as a link to the culture they have left and gently introduce the mores of the country they have just adopted.

The Contributions of the Private Sector

Special interest groups whose energies are channeled towards giving assistance to specific areas of need are often lumped together and called "the private sector." These groups are made up mainly of parent associations and other agencies which raise and distribute money and services on behalf of the developmentally disabled, the handicapped, or otherwise less privileged persons. Originally formed to publicize the problems and to research ways of meeting the needs of a particular population, these groups were often started by professionals dealing with educating or institutionalizing the disabled.

Prior to World War I, most social welfare agencies were privately run charitable societies, settlement houses, and philanthropic endeavors. The early workers in these agencies were mostly volunteers. Their responsibilities ranged from counseling individual clients to meeting with other agencies in order to plan more effective ways of helping groups of people. Settlement houses served, for the most part, to help the large immigrant populations settling in the cities to cope with poverty, disease, and estrangement. Community action movements often had their start in the settlement programs. Social work as a career evolved at this time.

From this time until the middle of the 20th century, social work continued to evolve as a distinct methodology reflecting the major philosophic and psychological trends. It attempted to solve the social problems caused by the Industrial Revolution, World War I, urbanization, the Great Depression, World War II, and the Korean War. At the same time, major improvements in medicine and technology—such as the improved survival rate of children with severe developmental problems—often served to magnify areas in which the aid of social services was needed.

Since few charitable agencies benefited from government money, there was intense competition for private funding sources. This was eventually ameliorated somewhat by the organization called the Community Chest. The Community Chest coordinated fund raising within a community and then divided the contributions among the participating agencies in a fair and equitable manner, according to the amount or degree of services provided by the agency to the community. Today, the Community Chest is known as the United Fund or the United Way.

Foundations and philanthropic organizations also developed during this time of intense social change. As nongovernmental agencies existing to serve the public, foundations usually make grants or donations to individuals or groups. Usually, but not always, endowed, foundations exist to distribute money or the income from invested money which has been set aside by some original donor or group of donors. They also may receive and disburse regular contributions.

Normally a foundation chooses one or more segments of public concern to aid, investigate, or improve. A foundation may also support action programs which are administrated by its own staff. Large foundations employ a whole spectrum of human service personnel or research scientists in addition to administrative staff.

Although foundations are generally called "private," they are in an interesting position. Once money has been given to a foundation, it no longer belongs to the original donor. It becomes public money which has been categorized for a specific purpose. In addition, all of the activities of a foundation are not private, but must, by law, be reported to the government. The decisions of foundations, however, are not made by the government or by the public. They are in the hands of the foundation administrators.

Diversity in the Private Sector

The diversity of private agencies is enormous. Sizes vary immensely—from the Ford Foundation whose holdings were valued at well over $3 billion in 1972 to foundations with hardly any assets at all. Larger foundations with assets of more than $4 or $5 million usually make grants and undertake programs which meet criteria developed on a systematic basis. Smaller organizations may distribute their income in a less organized and regulated manner while agencies of $100,000 or less often exist only as vehicles for individual benevolences. Although the nature and the size of the programs undertaken by the foundation are directly affected by the amount of assets available, the quality of the services rendered by the organization are not.

Some factors which can be determined by the size of the foundation are the methods used to determine decisions made by the foundation, the staffing of the foundation administration, and the areas that the foundation will sponsor.

Decisions about who shall receive grants are made in different ways by different foundations. There are some who have so many requests that only a small percentage of them can be honored. Other agencies are so small and relatively unknown that they receive no requests at all. In addition, whereas most foundations carefully research their grant requests and make their decisions according to a previously determined policy, there are others that end the year searching for grants to make in order to spend the money required by law.

Size also affects the staffing of foundations. While the small organizations employ only a few clerical workers and administrators, large foundations have huge networks of professionals, research people, legal departments, and advisory boards. The experience and quality of staff is not determined by size, nor is the competence of the people entrusted with decision-making.

Sponsorship is an additional area of difference. Although most foundations were established by a single person or family, their areas of concern may be permanently guided by a set of very narrow guidelines and original purposes, or they may be broadly defined and flexible enough to meet new challenges.

Foundations have one major factor in common regardless of size, geographic location, or the original idiosyncracies of the founder. They have no need to raise any money in order to maintain their own administration or to fund their programs. In this respect, they are different from other private charities and agencies that forever must be seeking donations to enable them to maintain their base of operations and perform their services. It is a happy marriage, therefore, when specific foundations espouse particular agencies whose programs are in line with the goals of the foundation.

The achievement record of foundations is impressive. The Carnegie Corporation, for instance, pays a great deal of financial attention to preschool and minority education. The television program "Sesame Street" is a notable success in this area. The Commonwealth Fund of New York City devotes much of its funds to medical education in the form of Harkness Fellowships and to problems of community health. The Danforth Foundation in St. Louis and the Duke Endowment in North and South Carolina support urban studies, secondary school and college programs, hospitals, and orphanages.

The Ford Foundation, always interested in social problems, funds legal aid programs, minority entrepreneurship, and many other human service needs. The Lilly Endowment in Indianapolis has programs of unrestricted grants to all of the private colleges and universities in Indiana as well as to programs devoted to community service. The Andrew Mellon Foundation aids many minority institutions of higher learning. The Rockefeller Brothers Fund devotes much of its attention to major social problems throughout the country as well as to urban problems and charities in New York City. The Rockefeller Foundation has made significant contributions to nearly every major needs area from world hunger to equal opportunity. This foundation works both through grants to organizations and through operations of its own.

These large foundations with their enormous grants are only a fraction of the organizations disbursing funds throughout the country. Although the majority of them are not actively involved in fieldwork or direct research, some foundations employ professionals in many different human service fields in administrative or evaluative positions.

Where the Jobs Are

Few people enter the field of human services with the goal of working for a foundation. Most of the contact human service professionals have with foundations is on the receiving end. The writing of grant requests is an important part of the training of most professionals who hope to move into administrative positions.

For the most part, churches and foundations, two of the largest agencies in the private sector, do not directly employ human service personnel. The bulk of their paid employees are largely administrative and clerical, and, in the case of religious organizations, most of the workers are volunteers.

Where are the jobs in private agencies? They are all around you. With the current emphasis on deinstitutionalization and the improvement of community services, jobs in the private sector are expected to increase.

The mood of the nation has swung from big government spending programs aimed at reducing or eradicating social problems to a much more conservative point of view. The current belief is that less government support and control of service programs leads to more efficiency. How successful the present administration will be in revitalizing traditions of volunteerism and returning the responsibility for the well-being of the public to community, state, and private control remains to be seen. Regardless of whether or not the New Federalism improves service delivery, there will be a greater emphasis on the responsibility of the private sector to meet the human service needs of the community.

It is hoped that the greater visibility of private agencies will focus attention on the disparity between the modest salaries earned by professionals who are protected by civil service regulations and the much lower salaries available to equally well-qualified professionals working in the private sector. The poor salaries often paid by private agencies are directly related to the constant need for money in order to exist as well as to pay personnel. The social work aide, as well as other paraprofessional workers, has helped many private and public agencies to provide more hands-on staff for less dollars.

There is an enormous variety of private agencies, all employing human service professionals in all categories. Local newspapers frequently run advertisements requesting teachers for church-sponsored schools, neighborhood day-care centers, and for the many day schools and camps specializing in services for the developmentally disabled or emotionally handicapped. Parent-sponsored organizations such as the Association for Children with Learning Disabilities and the Association for Retarded Children participate in and fund schools and therapy programs for handicapped children. These schools employ human service personnel in nearly all of the areas discussed in this book. There are also a vast number of residential schools and private institutions serving special populations.

Jobs in these agencies are very rewarding and provide excellent experience. They often allow a degree of freedom to try out new techniques and to achieve an exceptionally close working relationship with co-workers and clients.

Other important and crucially needed areas which often employ entry-level personnel are alcohol or drug rehabilitation programs, child abuse clinics, and crisis intervention and suicide centers. An additional new area to explore, especially for nurses, is the growing number of trauma centers. All of these jobs offer plenty of action and tax skills and stamina to the utmost. Nurses, psychologists, therapists of all kinds, and caseworkers may all be able to find jobs in these areas.

There are also three relatively recent developments in human services which employ many trained people in private agencies as well as in public ones. They are all in the process of exploring and expanding areas and methods of service and offer great promise for the future both as career areas and as exciting improvements in service.

Day-care programs for the aged are a new way of providing services to the growing numbers of people needing geriatric care without having to place them in expensive and demoralizing residential care situations. Agencies and centers providing day programs often employ creative therapists, physical therapists, nurses, nutritionists, psychologists, and casework counselors as well as paraprofessionals in all areas.

Neighborhood group homes and skill development homes are another example of the trend away from institutionalization and towards a normalized life for children and adults with special needs. There are group homes and community-based sheltered apartments designed to help many different disabled people to live in less restrictive environments than were formerly thought to be necessary. Retarded people and emotionally disturbed or physically disabled individuals are learning to live in community settings and use the services available to the community. There are also halfway homes for children who would otherwise be placed in correctional institutions. These homes are serviced by many private agencies employing special education teachers, nurses, social workers, therapists, counselors, and also frequently hiring consultants to provide in-service training to the professionals and paraprofessionals employed by these agencies.

The hospice movement is the third new area affecting programs in private agencies throughout the country. Although the movement utilizes large numbers of volunteers, their training is becoming more specific. Professionals in the fields of psychology, social work, counseling, the creative therapies, and nursing are all finding interesting and challenging ways to contribute to this field.

A list of private agencies to contact for career information may be found at the end of this book.

References

Cuninggim, M. *Private Money and Public Service.* McGraw-Hill Book Co., 1972.

Elder, J. "How The New Federalism Affects Developmental Disabilities." *Clearinghouse On the Handicapped.* Department of Education, Office of Information and Resources for the Handicapped. July/August 1982, No. 4.

The First Half Century 1930–1980; Private Approaches to Public Need. W.K. Kellogg Foundation, 1980.

Magreb, P., and Elder, J. *Planning for Services to Handicapped Persons: Community, Education, Health.* Paul H. Brookes Publishing Co., Inc., 1979.

Morales, A., and Sheafor, B. *Social Work: A Profession of Many Faces.* Allyn and Bacon, Inc., 1977.

Sloan, W., and Stevens, H. *A Century of Concern: A History of the American Association on Mental Deficiency.* A.A.M.D. Inc., 1976.

6. GOVERNMENT CAREERS IN THE HUMAN SERVICES

At the present time, there are more than 80,000 distinct branches of government in the United States. In addition to the many branches of federal and state government, each municipality in every county of every state is a separate governing agency. All of them are potential sources of employment for you if you choose a career in the human services. The bad news is that all of them are suffering from the problems of the current economic situation and are having to make substantial budget cuts.

The major challenge for the person planning a career in the human services today arises from the present economic situation in our country. There is a growing need for services at the precise time that large numbers of personnel are being cut from government payrolls. Just when the unemployment lines are getting longer and longer, the staff distributing the unemployment checks is being radically cut.

Unemployment, urbanization, computerization, and normalization are not just long words; they are conditions which are rapidly changing the nature of the present United States population in this decade.

Another anomaly is caused by the fact that improvements in technology, medical care, and educational training techniques have changed the type as well as the scope of services now provided to the disabled or the needy. So again, as more services are developed to improve the quality of life for a wide variety of human service clients, there are fewer people who can afford to pay for these services and fewer programs which are available to the needy at reduced cost or as a public service.

A streamlining of government is probably long overdue. Overlap in governmental services at all levels is wasteful to the taxpayer and confusing to the consumer. Every level of government is experiencing change as it refocuses its attention on new responsibilities and mobilizes its resources to deal with community problems in the 1980's.

However, in spite of the current economic picture, there are careers being created because new needs are emerging. An example of this can be seen in the current wave of attention being given to the needs of the aged now that Congress has passed the Older Americans Act. New job titles, such as geriatric technician, have begun to appear in government employment opportunity bulletins.

The current push towards deinstitutionalization has resulted in a movement to set up group homes, community centers, and apartments for individuals with special needs. Their staffs must have the skills and training to provide structure for these centers while teaching clients to assume control over their own lives and environments.

The future in government service careers holds the promise of much change. Since Americans have come to expect a wide variety of services from all levels of government, there is likely to be a continuing demand for public service workers despite continued cutbacks. The salaries and services of governmental human service agencies and organizations are all financed by taxes on income, sales, property, or inheritance. In some states, the agencies are recipients of monies derived from lotteries. Many privately run agencies, schools, and programs also derive a major portion of their budget from public revenues.

In this chapter, we will discuss the kinds of careers that are found in the public sector, the current influences determining their present nature, and their future direction. Some of these jobs are identical to careers found in the private sector; others exist only in government service. Some jobs are protected by civil service regulations while others are not. By far, the largest group of state and local employees, approximately 40 percent, is involved in some phase of public education.

The nature of government careers is in a state of flux because of the present combination of social, economic, political, and technological forces actively shaping the environment. We will briefly touch on these in order to gain some understanding of future needs.

Government career patterns, as complex and overlapping as they are, are divided by jurisdiction and management into three areas: local, state, and federal. We will explore major job titles

The habilitation plan coordinator follows up on clients placed in a group home. (Photo by Marlene Wiener)

that are currently available in each area. If you keep in mind which of the ten professional careers outlined in Chapter 2 appealed most to you, you will be able to see how they fit into the government structure and at which level they seem most challenging to you. You will also find suggestions for achieving career mobility within the government as well as sources to check for further information.

What Does the Future Hold for Government Careers?

One important criterion affecting the location of jobs as well as the nature of some careers is the continuing population shift to the Sun Belt. It is expected that, while other parts of the country will experience small or modest growth in this decade, the South and West will continue to boom.

Minority populations will continue to grow in the United States because of immigration policies and the number of illegal aliens who manage to enter the country. These groups continue to need many services to become contributors to the economy rather than drains upon its resources.

Before the end of the decade, the impact of a new generation of babies must be faced. There will be an increased need for people to educate, nurse, feed, and otherwise serve the needs of this large group, the majority of whom are ready to enter school.

Political changes, of course, have a direct effect upon the kind, amount, and quality of services available to the needy. The trend away from centralized government control and towards local and community solutions to social problems may change the locations of jobs and services. The economic healthiness of the country will determine whether there will be enough money to pay for them.

Technological change also has an impact on our employment patterns. It is hard to predict the implications for major employment fields such as agriculture, manufacturing, and science, but we appear to be moving towards a more service-oriented economy which will certainly affect the field of human services.

It is obvious that the one sure thing that the future will bring to government career opportunities is change.

Local and Community Services

This is the level where the most action is supposed to occur over the next few years. In these programs, you will get to deal directly with clients. Most large cities, and nearly every county, publish some form of directory every year or two listing the agencies and organizations which respond to human service needs at the community level. This directory will provide you with essential information on the location and variety of public and private service organizations providing assistance in your area. Information on job availability, necessary qualifications, and hiring procedures is often obtained by a quick phone call.

Glancing at the wide variety of available services will also provide you with a view of the different career opportunities within the structure of municipal and county government. You will find organizations that assist people in the areas of: alcoholism, day care, psychological counseling, drug abuse, elderly services, food stamps, aid to dependent children, services to the handicapped and the disabled, housing, unemployment and job training, support groups, legal services, and many more. Schools and institutions for children and adults with special needs will be listed as well as recreation centers, nursing homes, and clinics.

Entry-level jobs at local levels may require that you take a civil service examination in accordance with state procedures. It is a good idea to check the monthly job opportunities bulletins issued by state civil service commissions for current examinations being offered. These may usually be found in post offices, public libraries, state employment offices, and other state and municipal personnel offices.

Civil Service Examinations

If you are interested in career mobility, you should probably apply for as many civil service examinations as you are qualified to take. These examinations cover a wide variety of career fields and often allow you to substitute related experience in lieu of educational requirements. They can help you to move into higher-level jobs as well as to move laterally into different career areas. There are a number of different kinds of civil service examinations which may be offered to people wishing to work in government.

Open-competitive examinations are available to all people who meet the general qualifications listed in the announcement. There may or may not be a filing fee depending on the state in which you are living.

Continuous recruitment examinations are a specific form of open-competitive or promotional examination which usually require some kind of specific education and experience. They are different from other examinations in that applications are accepted continuously and tests are held more frequently. These examinations are given often because there is a continuing need to fill these positions.

Promotional examinations are tests which usually require you to be currently employed in a permanent, competitive job title. They are given as an opportunity for you to move to the next highest level in the system. Sometimes they are held on an interdepartmental basis in order to permit candidates to move to other agencies or organizations. Occasionally, employees in noncompetitive classes are eligible to compete in these examinations.

Other specifically designed examinations are sometimes offered to allow permanent employees to compete for professional, paraprofessional, or technical positions.

All of the examinations may consist of one or more of the following kinds of tests:

Written examinations are usually multiple-choice tests which are designed to measure the knowledge, skills, and other qualifications essential to job success.

Oral examinations are tests in which you will be questioned by a panel of experts. You will be requested to discuss your experience and qualifications for the job. This type of examination is given when the job requires the ability to speak well and to interact effectively with others. The panel will look for candidates who demonstrate confidence in their own expertise, awareness of the difficulties they may encounter, and eagerness to meet the challenges of the position. This kind of test is generally given at the higher administrative levels.

Education and experience tests are, in most cases, an evaluation of the type, amount, and dates of your education and work experience in areas pertinent to the job. If you meet the minimum qualifications you will receive a passing score. Higher ratings will depend on superior credentials.

Performance tests require candidates to actually perform a given set of tasks which are part of the job or to simulate tasks which are basic to successful job performance. An example of this would be a test for a clerical position in which you would actually have to demonstrate typing skills.

These tests are sometimes given in combination with other tests to provide a rounded picture of an applicant's abilities. Sometimes they are qualifying tests which means you either pass or fail. Your score, once you pass, is not used to determine whether you are hired. In weighted tests, your score is considered in your final mark.

It is important to note that volunteer and part-time experience is often counted in qualifying for an exam. There may be several ways to qualify for a test and you may often be permitted to substitute experience for education. Also, you may be employed provisionally in a position without taking any test at all. When a test is subsequently offered, you will have to take it but the experience you have gained while in the position will usually be of enormous help in passing the examination.

Community service agencies, whether public or private, are subject to state licensing regulations. Since most of them derive some of their funding from federal programs and grants, they usually must comply with federal regulations as well. This fact tends to standardize the requirements needed for employment in similar job categories, even when they are not subject to civil service classification.

State Positions in the Human Services

Each state has a department which functions as a major social service agency, providing services to all of the citizens of that state who qualify. This department, which may be entitled Department of Human Services, Department of Health and Human Services, etc., usually employs thousands of people.

A Department of Human Services is generally divided into sections providing specific services as follows:

Services to the Blind and Visually Impaired

This division provides services which include counseling, medical treatment, education, training, and job placement. It also may participate in state and federal vocational rehabilitation programs and home industries.

Human service professionals employed by this division include social workers, special education teachers, and occupational and rehabilitation therapists. Also found on the staffs of various state schools for the blind are psychologists, art, dance, or music therapists, and speech and language pathologists. Many counseling services are provided to newly blinded individuals and to blind children and adults as they enter into school and community settings.

Medical Assistance and Health Services (Medicaid)

These are joint federal and state programs that serve the medical and health needs of the poor. They consist of inpatient and outpatient hospital care, skilled nursing and intermediate care, home health care, medical day care, early and periodic screening, pharmaceutical assistance to the aged, diagnosis and treatment for children, mental health clinic services, and family planning. There are employment opportunities for all human service professionals in the programs provided by this division.

Mental Health and Hospitals

This division usually administers state psychiatric hospitals, adolescent and child residential programs, special facilities for geriatric patients, and many transitional services. It also assists in the development and funding of community mental health centers, clinics, deinstitutionalization programs, and rehabilitation services. Program evaluation as well as the provision and coordination of public education programs concerning mental health may also be included in the programs provided by this division.

Mental Retardation/Developmental Disabilities

This division provides functional services to the developmentally disabled, including administrating and operating institutions and other residential facilities for the retarded, purchase of other residential care, day training programs for children, adult activity centers, guardianship, regional social services, community functions such as field services and group residences, respite care services, special education services, services to deaf-blind retardates, and comprehensive long-range planning and needs-assessment programs. The entire range of human service professionals and paraprofessionals are employed in this division.

Public Welfare

This is the division which administers public assistance programs such as Aid to Families With Dependent Children, General Assistance, food stamps, home energy assistance, and refugee assistance programs. These programs are administered at the local level.

Veterans Programs and Special Services

This is the bureau that assists veterans with the state and federal benefits to which they may be entitled. It also administers nursing homes for elderly or disabled veterans.

Youth and Family Services

This division administers many programs such as adoption and foster care placement, protective services for children who are abandoned, neglected, or abused, counseling and casework services to families, protective services for adults, foster grandparent programs, day-care services, and institutional and community residential placements.

Since each state is unique in serving populations whose needs may be very different, the department offering health and human service care will be designed to provide assistance with the problems arising and existing in the state. Agricultural states will provide services that may be quite different from urban, industrial states, or states with large native American or Mexican populations.

Employment opportunities at the state level are posted in all state agencies and published in major newspapers. Since most of the positions have civil service classifications, you may have to take an examination in your job title before you are eligible to apply for the position. You should always read a job description carefully, as well as the requirements for the job, because different states, departments, or facilities may use different titles for the same job.

Human Service Opportunities in th
Government

128

The federal government has many emplo[
for those who are interested in human servi
its departments such as the Department of
Services or the Department of Education a
explore, but there are also many interesting jobs available to
the human service professional in other government departments.

Many pertinent federal employers are listed here but it would
be impossible to list them all. Agencies and departments re-
organize constantly as they attempt to adjust to current trends
or to legislative or executive action.

The United States Government Organization Manual contains
descriptions of all the agencies of the branches of government.
Copies of this manual are available for 75 cents from:

> The Superintendent of Documents
> Government Printing Office
> Washington, DC 20402

Human Service Job Titles

Contact Representatives provide information, advice, and
assistance to veterans, their beneficiaries, and other interested
persons. They help to see that rights, benefits, privileges, or
obligations are carried out under the laws administered by the
Veterans Administration (V.A.). They help to prepare and present claims and advise veterans on services that are provided to
them by other agencies. At higher administrative levels, they
may direct, supervise, or administer all types of public contact
work.

The V.A. employs over 3500 contact representatives. Each
year there may be as many as 400 entry-level vacancies. A
bachelor's degree in any major field of study will qualify you for
this position.

Correction Officers have a great opportunity to effect social
change by playing an important role in influencing the attitudes
and actions of imprisoned offenders. They also help inmates to
develop skills and good work habits so that they can find and
maintain jobs after they are released.

rrection officers work in the correctional institutions of the
.S. Bureau of Prisons. They are responsible for maintaining
the confinement, safety, health, and protection of prisoners. They
supervise work projects and counsel individuals on goals and
family problems. They work closely with social workers, psychologists, teachers, and other members of the treatment team
to help change the behavior pattern of the convicted offender.

Opportunities for advancement in this field are good and may
lead to higher-level positions.

Qualifications: Four years of college plus six months of appropriate experience will qualify you for an entry-level position.

Correctional Treatment Specialists may work in correctional
institutions, in the central office of the Bureau of Prisons, in the
District of Columbia Department of Corrections or with the
United States Board of Parole. The job is involved with the
development, evaluation, and analysis of diagnostic information
and data concerning inmates. They may prepare social histories
and recommend programs of education, counseling, vocational
training, and work to the institutional classification committee.
They evaluate progress and make recommendations to the Board
of Parole about an offender's possible adjustment to the community. They work with prisoners, their families, probation
officers, and social agencies. Opportunities for advancement are
excellent.

Qualifications: Four years of college study with at least 24
hours in the social sciences, plus two years of appropriate experience, two years of graduate study, or completion of requirements for a master's degree.

Employment Assistance Specialists work at the Bureau of
Indian Affairs in the Department of the Interior. They assist
Indians who wish to relocate from reservations to communities
where chances for employment may be better. These specialists
help in exploring employment opportunities, providing financial
assistance for moving, and otherwise aiding the Indian family
to adjust to community life.

Qualifications: A bachelor's degree in any major field is the
only requirement. Study in related fields such as anthropology,
psychology, sociology, or social work will be helpful.

Food Program Specialists are responsible for the development,
promotion, and evaluation of programs concerned with providing
food to low-income families, disaster victims, schools, and non-
profit institutions. Specialists work in cooperation with state
and local agencies and community organizations. Some specialists

are involved with the management of food stamp programs, food distribution, school lunch programs, and child nutrition programs.

Qualifications: A degree in any major field of study is the only requirement. Study in social work, administration, and nutrition will be very helpful.

Manpower Development Specialists are employed by the Department of Labor to administer and participate in the development and assessment of a comprehensive program designed to provide the underemployed and the unemployed with skills that will enable them to participate in the labor force. Specialists work to improve the employability of unemployed youth, school dropouts, and others who need continued education in order to succeed.

Some manpower specialists are concerned with general problems while others deal with specific areas of the program.

Qualifications: A bachelor's degree which includes 24 semester hours in one or more of the social sciences is necessary for entry into this field.

Psychologists in the federal service usually work in very specialized areas such as personnel measurement and evaluation, and clinical, counseling, or social psychology. They may deal with educational, vocational, and personal adjustment counseling and study the psychological aspects of fatigue, perception, and learning. In addition, they may standardize devices for measuring job performance or investigate adjustments to group living, such as military life.

Opportunities for placement and advancement are good as there are over 2000 psychologists employed by the federal service. Most of the positions are located in the V.A. and in the Departments of the Air Force, Army, Navy, Health and Human Services, and Education.

Qualifications: At the entrance grade, some positions require only four years of college study with 24 hours in psychology and at least one course in statistics. The majority of positions, however, are filled at a higher grade requiring: for counseling psychologists, two years of graduate study plus one year of counseling experience; for clinical psychologists, a Ph.D. plus an internship.

Recreation Specialists evaluate the recreation needs of military personnel and their dependents, the ill and handicapped in hospitals, and residents of the District of Columbia. They plan, organize, and supervise recreation programs which may include arts and crafts, dramatics, music, sports, etc., in order to provide constructive uses for leisure time or to supplement rehabilitation programs.

These specialists are employed by the V.A., the Armed Services, the Department of Health and Human Services, and the Department of Education. There are well over 2000 of these specialists in the federal government. There are opportunities within this career field for positions overseas as well as in the United States.

Qualifications: Four years of college study with a major in an appropriate area such as recreation, recreation therapy, physical education, dramatic arts, music, vocational and industrial arts, art, education, or sociology.

Social Workers may work on an Indian reservation, in an inner-city office, or in many other settings. Most are involved with direct casework but there are also opportunities to work with communities or to participate in the development and administration of social health programs.

There is a continuing need for qualified persons in this field. Entrance positions in public assistance are located in the District of Columbia. Other positions are located throughout the country in the V.A. and the Departments of Justice, Defense, Interior, Education, Correction, and Health and Human Services.

Qualifications: For the regular entrance grade, applicants must have completed all the requirements for a master's degree in social work. Applicants may qualify for higher-level positions if their second year of graduate study included two semesters or three quarters of supervised fieldwork or casework in a hospital, clinic, family service, or child or public welfare agency.

Educators may be found counseling in government-sponsored schools or education programs, advising on programs, or giving guidance to educational and cultural agencies. They may also administer school programs, supervise teaching staff members, or assist in developing audio-visual aids. There are over 30,000 educators employed by the federal government. Positions may be found in many different agencies but the major employers are the Departments of Defense, Interior, Labor, Justice, Corrections, Education, and Health and Human Services.

The Bureau of Indian Affairs in the Department of the Interior employs teachers to educate Indian children and adults who are not served by public schools. Classroom teachers and guidance counselors are especially needed as are special education teachers.

The Bureau of Prisons in the Department of Justice employs teachers for remedial reading as well as for academic and vocational subjects. Teachers may also be involved in recreation, guidance, administrative work, and research.

Job Corps teachers are employed by the Department of Labor to teach basic academic and vocational skills to unemployed adolescents.

A large number of teachers are employed by the Department of Defense. Language instructors teach military personnel but the majority of teachers are employed in the United States and 27 other countries to provide educational services to the children of military and civilian personnel who live overseas.

Qualifications: Standards may vary considerably for some positions but, in general, 18 hours of education or more are required. In addition, most positions now require experience or further educational requirements.

Dieticians are employed mainly in hospitals and outpatient clinics. They perform a full range of professional dietetic services ranging from program management, casework services, education, and research to designing programs to meet the changing nutritional needs of patients.

Opportunities in this area are good. More than 1000 dieticians are employed by the federal government working mainly in the V.A., and the Department of Health and Human Services.

Qualifications: Dieticians must have a bachelor's degree in a curriculum approved by the American Dietetic Association. In order to enter at a higher grade, you must complete a hospital, clinic, college, or commercial internship approved by the A.D.A.

Nurses employed by the federal government fall into three categories:

1. Clinical nurses provide traditional care for patients in a hospital setting or work in educational, administrative, or clinical positions at public health service hospitals or the V.A.

2. Public health nurses visit homes, schools, and clinics to provide care for the sick and lead training programs in prevention and health care. They work mainly in health and human service areas.

3. Occupational health nurses provide health services to the employees of federal agencies and installations.

Employment opportunities are excellent. There are more than 20,000 nurses working in the federal government. Nearly 2000 vacancies are filled each year at entry-level. Positions exist in all of the states as well as overseas.

Qualifications: All applicants for nurse positions must also have an active current registration as a professional nurse in a state, the District of Columbia, Puerto Rico, or territories of the United States.

Nurses (Veterans Administration) are registered nurses in the V.A. involved with treatment in areas such as intensive care, alcohol and drug treatment, coronary care, hemodialysis, respiratory care, extended care, gerontology, spinal cord injury, nurse administered units, and ambulatory care. There are opportunities for nurse practitioners as well as clinical specialists. There are 171 V.A. hospitals, most of which are medical and surgical facilities. Several of them provide psychiatric facilities as well.

V.A. hospitals employ more than 23,000 registered nurses. More than 5000 nurses are hired each year.

V.A. nurses are appointed at one of several grades depending on the extent and nature of their education and experience. No civil service examination is required.

Occupational Therapists are employed in hospitals throughout the United States. They provide a full range of services to patients having tuberculosis, general medical or surgical problems, or neurological or psychiatric conditions.

They are employed mainly by the V.A. and Departments of Defense and Health and Human Services.

Qualifications: Applicants must have graduated from a school of occupational therapy approved by the Council on Medical Education and Hospitals. They must also have completed the clinical requirements prescribed by the school granting the degree.

Physical Therapists are hired by the federal government to administer or supervise treatment of patients. They also perform tests to determine muscle, nerve, and skin conditions and conduct special training.

Principal employers are the V.A., Department of Health and Human Services, and agencies of the Defense Department.

Qualifications: Applicants must have graduated from a school of physical therapy approved by the American Medical Association and have completed the clinical affiliation requirements.

Speech Pathologists and Audiologists work with communicative disorders through research, consultation, and training at outpatient facilities and in hospitals. They are primarily concerned with the rehabilitation of veterans and military personnel. They test hearing acuity, select, fit, and train patients in the use of hearing aids, train patients to lip-read and to use sign language, and administer speech and language programs designed to help clients regain or retain intelligible speech.

This is a comparatively new professional area within the federal government but it is expanding with a demand for well-trained persons. The V.A. and military agencies are the major employers of this specialty.

Qualifications: Applicants must have a master's degree in either speech pathology or audiology which includes at least 18 hours in the field. In order to be eligible for a higher-level position, the master's program must have consisted of at least three semester hours of academic training and 335 clock hours of clinical training.

Applying for a Federal Position

In order to be considered for employment with a federal agency, it is necessary to make formal application through the Civil Service Commission so that eligibility may be determined. This may be done at the nearest Federal Job Information Center or at a Commission office.

Upon receiving a rating from the Civil Service Commission, the applicant is placed on an appropriate list for qualification. These lists are established as the result of a competitive examination. Although some of the examinations require tests, others rate the applicant on the basis of experience and education as shown on the application form.

The Civil Service Commission functions through area offices which are located in centers of population throughout the country.

Addresses of these centers may be obtained by writing to:

United States Civil Service Commission
Civil Service Commission Building
1900 E Street, NW
Washington, DC 20415

These addresses as well as other job announcements and literature issued by the Civil Service Commission may be available in your local high school or college guidance and placement offices. Also, check the U.S. government listing in your telephone directory for agencies and Federal Job Information Centers near you.

You will receive faster answers to your employment questions if you contact field offices of federal agencies rather than the Washington, DC office.

Employment Opportunities

Most positions in the federal government are classified into grade levels of the General Schedule (G.S.) according to the difficulty as well as the responsibilities of the job. A salary range is assigned to each grade and fixed by Congress.

In the Federal Salary Reform Act of 1962, Congress declared that federal salaries shall be competitive with those of private enterprise for the same levels of work.

Additional Information

For additional information, address inquiries as follows:

Information on jobs involving food and nutrition

Employment Branch
Personnel Division
Food and Nutrition Service
U.S. Department of Agriculture
Washington, DC 20250

Information on human service positions in the U.S. Army

Director
Army Employment Coordination Service
Office of the Secretary of the Army
Room 1A 111, The Pentagon
Washington, DC 20310

Information on jobs in the Department of Health and Human Services

Office of the Secretary
Personnel Office
Department of Health and Human Services
330 Independence Avenue, SW
Washington, DC 20201

Listed below are the ten regional offices of this department:

Regional Personnel Officer
HHS Region I
JFK Federal Building
Government Center
Boston, MA 02203

Regional Personnel Officer
HHS Region II
Federal Building
26 Federal Plaza
New York, NY 10007

Regional Personnel Officer
HHS Region III
P.O. Box 13716
Philadelphia, PA 19101

Regional Personnel Officer
HHS Region IV
Peachtree-Seventh Building
50 Seventh Street, NE
Atlanta, GA 30323

Regional Personnel Officer
HHS Region V
300 South Wacker Drive
35th Floor
Chicago, IL 60607

Regional Personnel Officer
HHS Region VI
1114 Commerce Street
Dallas, TX 75202

Regional Personnel Officer
HHS Region VII
Federal Office Building
601 East 12th Street
Kansas City, MO 64108

Regional Personnel Officer
HHS Region VIII
Federal Office Building
19th and Stout Streets
Denver, CO 80202

Regional Personnel Officer
HHS Region IX
Federal Office Building
50 Fulton Street
San Francisco, CA 94102

Regional Personnel Officer
HHS Region X
1321 Second Avenue
Arcade Plaza
Seattle, WA 98101

Information about jobs in the Department of the Interior

Director
Bureau of Indian Affairs
Department of the Interior
Washington, DC 20240

Information about jobs in the Justice Department
Director
Personnel and Training Staff
Department of Justice
Washington, DC 20530

Personnel Officer
Bureau of Prisons
101 Indiana Avenue, NW
Washington, DC 20537

Information about jobs in the Department of Labor
Office of Special Personnel Services
Directorate of Personnel Management
New Department of Labor Building
Washington, DC 20210

Information about jobs in the Department of Education
Office of Personnel Services
U.S. Department of Education
Washington, DC 20202

References

Department of Health, Education and Welfare. *Federal Assistance for Programs Serving the Handicapped*. Office for Handicapped Individuals, September 1977.

Hawaii State Planning Council on Developmental Disabilities. *Projects That Work*. Hawaii State Department of Health, 1982.

New Jersey Department of Civil Service. *November Job Opportunities in State and Local Government*. Civil Service Commission, November 1982.

New Jersey Department of Human Services. *Human Services Reporter*. Vol. 4, No. 5, January 1982.

New Jersey Department of Human Services. *Manual of Standards for Child Care Centers*. January 1981.

New Jersey Public Information Office. *The Human Services Connection*. Department of Human Services, January 1982.

New York State Governor's Office of Employee Relations/Civil Service Employees Association, Joint Labor Management Committee on the Work Environment and Productivity. *Career Mobility*. June 1981.

Sandahl, E. (Ed.-in-Chief). *Up Front; The Newspaper for Handicapped and Disabled Persons*. UPF Inc., Vol. 2, No. 5, January 1982.

United States Civil Service Commission. *Federal Career Directory*. U.S. Government Printing Office, 1977.

U.S. Department of Health and Human Services. "It's Time to Tell" in *A Media Handbook for Human Services Personnel*. Office of Human Development Services and the Office of Family Assistance, 1980.

7. ADMINISTRATIVE CAREERS

Administrative careers in the field of human services are as varied as are the services provided by the enormous number of agencies, departments, and public and private organizations which attempt to meet the needs of American society. Each of the professional areas discussed in this book may well lead to an administrative position once you become experienced in your chosen field.

Administrators are the people who direct, guide, and assist the human service worker who deals directly with the client. Ideally, the administration of an agency strives to hire the most qualified staff, provide services to the greatest possible number of clients, and spend the least possible amount of money in order to accomplish this.

In a small agency, such as a local day-care center, the entire staff may consist of a head teacher, two or three assistants, a secretary-bookkeeper, and a janitor. In this case, the teacher is the agency administrator even though she may also have to answer to another administrator in a funding agency or a board of directors.

Many professionals with years of experience, demonstrated excellence, and advanced education in the field prefer to work at the contact level with clients. Others find that they possess qualities and skills in management areas. Such management positions which allow them to have an impact on policy may give them a greater sense of fulfillment.

Within government agencies and departments, a move from line to administrative positions is accomplished after you have achieved a certain degree of experience and, often, additional education in your field. You may also be required to take a civil service performance test before you can apply for a promotion or job change. In this way, a social worker, nurse, or teacher may move, not only from a starting level to an advanced level, but also to a supervisory position. The higher administrative positions, such as department head or director, may be appointive rather than promotional.

In the private sector, advancement may be surprisingly fast or extremely slow, depending on the nature and size of the agency as well as its staffing policies. The majority of large organizations, however, are very similar in structure to public agencies in that they often must meet certain staffing or other requirements before they are entitled to government funds.

In the larger agencies and organizations, there are often administrative positions or departments created in order to improve the performance or service the needs of the agency staff. Positions may also be created to broaden the services provided by the facility. Thus, there may be career opportunities available to human service professionals within staff training departments, program development and monitoring agencies, and consultant services.

In the fields of mental retardation, mental health, and services to the aged, there are many training programs for people who wish to run halfway houses, group homes, day-care programs, and supervised apartment facilities. These programs are designed to upgrade the care provided to the client by training care givers in areas as diverse as behavior management techniques, budgeting and marketing, and providing positive social experiences.

Management Skills

At the beginning of this book, we identified a number of qualities as being associated with success in human service. In the same way, there are skills which seem to be necessary or desirable if you are contemplating an administrative position. They fall into three major areas:

1. Highly developed interpersonal qualities such as: leadership, sensitivity, responsiveness, initiative, risk-taking, tenacity, and good stress tolerance.

2. Skills in managing such as: planning and organizing, delegating skills, problem solving techniques, decisiveness, and objectivity.

3. Good oral and written communication skills.

There are often management training programs provided to administrative personnel in order to develop and strengthen skills considered essential to good human service management.

It is not enough, however, to possess the traits often found in good managers. You must also have high performance goals for yourself as well as your staff, a thorough grounding in your field of expertise, and the ability to motivate yourself and your staff.

Most professions in the human services offer career ladders as well as mobility. When moving laterally or to a different job title, you may have to take an initial salary cut until you establish yourself. An exception to this is teaching, where tenure policies often serve to discourage movement. The scarcity of jobs at the present time is a further inducement not to move from an employment situation.

New Directions in Human Service Administration

The current trend towards moving health and human service care out of institutions and into the community is economically attractive to public and private agencies. Although there are sometimes problems with moving retarded or mentally ill individuals into community settings, there are two new alternatives to hospital or institutional care that appear to be well-received by the general public. These two programs offer services to families who have aged or terminally ill members in need of more care than the family is able to provide. Both programs, at present, seek to keep administrative costs as low as possible.

Hospices

A hospice is a place which provides care for terminally ill patients humanely and cheaply. The hospice movement began as an attempt to make a patient as comfortable as possible, surrounded by family, friends, warm and understanding nurses, and other care staff so that his last days are as nontraumatic as possible, for him as well as for those who love him. Treatment provided is generally nontraditional in that the usual chemotherapy, radiation, operations, and life-support systems are not provided. The staff seeks, as far as possible, to keep the patient pain-free and provides psychological counseling to the family as well as the client in order to help them to face and accept death as an inevitable part of life.

Costs are kept to a minimum because medical treatments and care are simplified and because the hospice utilizes family, friends, and volunteers as care givers in addition to nurses and therapists trained in the hospice movement.

Working in the hospice program is a very specialized career choice and demands a strong and stable personality with a high degree of dedication. If you feel you would be interested in knowing more about the program, it would be a good idea to seek out people involved with a local program. There are also a growing number of books on the subject. Your local librarian may be able to recommend several for you to read.

Day Care for the Aged

The other new program gaining public attention and support is the provision of daytime care and programming for the aged. This program is designed to serve two major groups of people: the aged individual who lives alone and appears to have few or no social contacts, and the aged or physically disabled person who lives at home with relatives and is unable to care for himself.

Typically, the person is picked up at home each day, transported to the facility, provided with nursing and social services, a hot lunch, and a daily activity program including recreational programs as well as occupational therapy. Charges for the service may be reimbursed by Medicaid.

One of the major benefits of the program is that people are able to continue to live in their own homes instead of having to enter residential nursing homes. There are psychological, social, and economic benefits to the client and to his family.

This program is still so new that administrative procedures are not firmly structured. Anyone interested in a career in the rapidly developing area of service to our growing population of elderly people should find this program very rewarding. These programs are run by private, religious, and public agencies. Licensing requirements are in the process of being set by the various states.

Human service professionals needed in this area include dieticians, nurses, occupational and creative therapists, audiologists and speech therapists, physical therapists, counselors, and recreational experts.

In addition, social workers are often needed to assist in identifying recipients and providing them with services.

This can be a very rewarding program for all who participate in it because it aims at building and restoring morale, maintaining the best possible health and nutrition, keeping the client in his own locale, and encouraging him to use his mind and his body in positive activities.

8. FINDING THE RIGHT JOB

If you have read this far, you are well on your way to taking the first steps toward finding the right career for you. Only you can decide which of the career options covered in this book meet your particular needs. If you have decided on one certain profession, then your next step should be to find out as much as possible about that particular career.

You must then develop a realistic career plan for yourself. This is accomplished by identifying both your long and short range goals. Ask yourself what courses or programs you will need to achieve your chosen profession. Investigate the schools which offer accredited programs. Discuss with your family and faculty adviser the amounts of time and money necessary to achieve your goal.

Having identified your goals, consider your particular strengths and weaknesses. Be as objective as you can in trying to see how they relate to your ability to reach your goals. Have you had, or can you get, volunteer or part-time experience that will help you to qualify for a position within your chosen career area?

Compare your goals with your strengths and weaknesses. Decide upon the course of action that will work best for you. If you have taken college courses related to your career objective, you may be able to pursue some options immediately. Otherwise, you should plan and carry out a program of study leading to a degree and certification or licensing in your chosen field.

It is a good idea to arrange to visit places where you think you would like to work. Hospitals, institutions, schools, and many agencies, public and private, will arrange a day for you to come and visit if you call and explain why you wish to make an observation.

Once you have explored the field and prepared to meet all the qualifications for entering it, you should study the newspapers and job opportunities bulletins that advertise jobs in your career area.

Letter of Application

When applying for a job, your letter of application is very important because it is the first contact your prospective employer will have with you. Your letter should be neatly typed and your spelling and grammar should be accurate. The letter should include the following information: your name, address, and phone number; a declaration of interest in the position being offered; a request for an interview; a copy of your resume.

The application should be short and direct and addressed to the person named in the advertisement or listed as the personnel director. A sample letter of application can be found on the next page.

Resume

A resume is an essential tool for anyone applying for a position as a human service professional. It is an effective method of presenting clear and concise information to the employer. Sending your resume with your letter of application helps to provide an employer with information about your preparation and experience in the field prior to your employment interview. Generally, when a great many people apply for one position, the information presented in the submitted resumes will determine whether or not the applicant is granted an interview. For this reason, it is important that your resume be constructed carefully so that the employer feels that your education and experience are exactly right for the job.

There are a number of resume styles you can use to present your qualifications. If you possess a strong educational background and have excellent working experience, it is probably most effective to list these facts as simply as possible, including certifications, honors, publications, etc.

If you are a recent graduate without much work experience in related areas, then it may be more effective to include a brief listing or description of strengths and abilities you possess that you feel will be needed in the job for which you are applying. If you have volunteer experience in the field, it is important to include it. Also included should be work experience that may be unrelated to the field but will point up specific skills such as

5 Smith Street
North East, MA   01069
(413) 222-3333

September 1, 1983

Mr. John Jones
Personnel Director
North East Developmental Center
North East, MA   01069

    I am very interested in applying for the position of Music Teacher which was advertised in the <u>Boston Times</u> on Sunday August 28, 1983.

    For the past five years I have been working as a music therapist in a developmental center in New York State. I believe my experience will be of benefit to your music program and would like to interview for the position.

    A copy of my resume is attached.

                  Sincerely,

                  Martha Smith

management ability, organization skills, and other positive qualities.

This resume style may also be suitable for someone reentering the job market after years at home raising a family. It is important to show that many of the skills needed in running a home and providing services to family and community can be transferred to employment in the human service areas. At the end of this chapter are several sample resumes for you to study.

There are many books available on effective resume writing. Most of them will give you good advice on the best style to use for the job you are seeking. It is wise, however, when applying for positions in health and human service areas, to avoid using "gimmicks" such as brightly colored paper, off-sized paper, or unusual kinds of script. These attention-getting methods may be very effective in the business or advertising world but they are not successful in most professional areas.

It has become more common for people to have resumes printed by professional printers. These resumes are generally very attractive and easy to read. The only drawback is that they give the employer the impression that you are applying for a great many positions. Some of the experts who give advice on resume writing recommend that each resume you send should be an original copy slanted towards one particular job.

Interviewing for the Job

Once you have been contacted for a job interview, you can probably surmise that your resume has presented you as someone with the right qualifications for the job. During the interview you will have the opportunity to discuss specifics about yourself and about the position. It will be helpful for you to spend some time thinking about the questions you may be asked and preparing the sort of answers you feel will present you in a positive way. Be prepared to discuss why you want this particular job.

There are a number of behaviors that will help you to demonstrate a good image. They are common to all successful job interviews, and are listed here for your review:

1. Be well-groomed. Wear comfortable clothing appropriate for the interview.

2. Plan to arrive at least ten minutes early.

3. Indicate your eagerness by walking briskly into the interview room.

4. Introduce yourself when meeting the interviewer and refer to him by name.

5. Indicate that you are interested in the job by being an alert and attentive listener.

6. Allow the interviewer to control the interview by leading the discussion.

7. Answer all questions directly but remember to use good judgment if you feel that a question is too personal.

8. Be ready to present diplomas or certificates so that the interviewer can verify the facts you have put in your resume.

9. Be courteous and maintain eye contact when talking to the interviewer.

10. Stress your qualifications for the job.

11. Try to be as natural as you can. If you are a bit nervous, the interviewer will probably excuse it.

12. Wait until the interviewer brings up the subject of salary before discussing wages.

Having a successful interview will depend on how effectively you are able to present yourself and your qualifications to the employer. There are many books available dealing with interviewing and presenting yourself effectively. Your librarian is an excellent source of information on the most up-to-date material.

If this book has piqued your interest in pursuing a career in one of the areas of human service, you will be entering into a very rewarding career field. In most cases, the rewards are not material. You will, however, experience the excitement and challenge that is part of the process of effecting change. You may be working with a single child or with many people in a community. You may deal with healing muscles or finding homes for needy families. You will be praised and loved at times. And at other times you will feel frustrated and ineffective. Always, however, you will find yourself needed and busy . . . and usually right where the action is!

References

Tesolowski, D.G., Ed.D. *Job Readiness Training Curriculum.* Materials Developmental Center, University of Wisconsin, Stout-Menomonie, WI, 1979.

Following are two resumes from recent college graduates seeking first professional employment.

Direct Style

SUSAN SMITH
67 Pine Street
Smalltown, New Jersey 07066
(201) 367-2233

OBJECTIVE

To secure a position as a teacher of the handicapped.

EDUCATION AND CERTIFICATION

B.A. Kean College of New Jersey, Union, New Jersey, 1982
Major: Early Childhood Education G.P.A. - 3.4/4.0

New Jersey State Certifications:
Elementary School Teacher - 1982
Teacher of the Handicapped - 1982
Nursery School Teacher - 1983

EXPERIENCE

Supplemental Instructor. Wilbur Developmental Center,
Wilbur, New Jersey. June 1982 to Present.
Duties include assisting head teacher in sensory stimulation
program for young, profoundly retarded children.

Instructor. Summer Day Camp for Retarded Children,
Smalltown, New Jersey. 1977 to 1981.
Worked summers during college with small groups of trainable
and moderately retarded teenagers. Was responsible for arts
and crafts program and worked on Special Olympics team.

REFERENCES

Supplied on request

Indirect Style

```
                        MARY JONES
                     2 Chestnut Street
                 Littletown, New Jersey  07009
                      (201) 239-7682


                          OBJECTIVE

Seeking challenging social service position working with the mentally
retarded in a group home or an institution.


                          EDUCATION

B.A. Montclair State College, Upper Montclair, New Jersey.  1963
     Major:  Psychology

Additional Coursework and Certifications:

     Teacher of the Handicapped certification at Montclair State
     College.  22 credits leading to the M.A. program in Special
     Education.  1980 - 1982

     New Jersey Certificate:  Teacher of the Handicapped.  1982


                      SKILLS AND ABILITIES

     Ability to assess needs
     Effective listening skills
     Patience and perseverance
     Excellent verbal and written communication skills
     Ability to coordinate services and activities
     Energetic and enthusiastic
     Experienced with infant stimulation programs
     Adaptable to change


                          EXPERIENCE

1963 - 1968:  Worked with mentally retarded and neurologically
handicapped children at Wilbur State Hospital for the Retarded.
I was in charge of planning physical education programs for
ambulatory as well as nonambulatory children with a broad range
of disabilities.  I also was part of the crisis intervention team
from 1966 to 1968.  I participated in a week-long state run crisis
intervention workshop in the summer of 1966.

1968 - Present:  I am running a household and mothering a family
of five children.  As a member of the local Cerebral Palsy Parents
Association, I have been very active in local programs serving
handicapped children in the community.  I also have served on the
board of directors of the county Association for Retarded Children.


References supplied upon request.
```

Resume of an Experienced Professional Seeking a Career Change

---

JANE ANN DOE
111 Smith Street
Littletown, New Jersey
(201) 111-2324

Goal
To improve services to the communicatively handicapped through efficient management, program development, and staff training.

Education
Master of Arts, 1979 (Audiology)
Kean College of New Jersey, Union, New Jersey

Bachelor of Arts, 1970 (Special Education)
Jersey City State College, Jersey City, New Jersey

Advanced Level Sign Language Training, 1982
Millburn School for the Hearing Handicapped, Millburn, New Jersey

Certifications
American Speech-Language-Hearing Association, 1981
   *Certificate of Clinical Competence

New Jersey State Department of Education, 1970
   *Teacher of the Handicapped
   *Speech Correctionist K-12
   *Teacher of the Blind and Partially Sighted

Employment History
Woodbridge State School, Woodbridge, New Jersey

   *Speech Therapist I   1979 to Present
   *Speech Therapist II   1971 to 1979
   *Speech Therapist Trainee   1970 to 1971

Responsible for:

Screening and diagnostic audiological evaluation of mentally retarded/multi-handicapped population;

Case presentations on residents referred to consulting audiologist and otologist, as well as assisting during those evaluations;

Developing and conducting a variety of staff training programs including sign language, care of hearing aids, audiological and impedance testing, communicative significance of hearing loss, and auditory training activities;

Improving communication skills of deaf/blind residents, which includes speech and language assessment, case review at evaluation meetings, writing individualized programs, and conducting therapy;

Consulting with professional and nonprofessional
staff to develop effective communication programs.

Millburn School for the Hearing Handicapped,
Millburn, New Jersey

*Instructor (part-time)   Fall 1982 to Present

Responsible for conducting Beginner I Level
Sign Language Program, which includes teaching
children and adults the basic skills necessary
for more advanced signing.

**Other Related
Experience and
Accomplishments**

Consulting

*Under contract with SPIN Enterprises, Inc.,
Philadelphia, provided consultation, evaluation,
and a written report for two clients. Project
involved a Total Communication Assessment and
hearing aid review. (Winter 1980)

*Served on two evaluation teams to assess speech,
language, and hearing of mentally retarded patients
confined to two New Jersey mental health facilities,
Essex County Psychiatric Hospital (1978) and Marlboro
State Hospital (1974).

Publications

*One Step at a Time: Visual, Auditory, and
Language Activities for the Deaf/Blind Child,
published by New Jersey State Commission for the
Blind in cooperation with Mid-Atlantic-North and
Caribbean Regional Deaf-Blind Center, 1977.
Collaborated on and wrote sections of chapter on
auditory skills.

*Manual for Language Development: A Handbook
of Strategies for Teaching Children Whose
Communicative Skills Range from Nonresponsive to
Use of Academic Language, published by Mid-
Atlantic-North and Caribbean Regional Deaf-Blind
Center, 1975. Collaborated on and wrote sections
of "Level IV: The Child Who Pushes and Pulls with
Situational Clues."

Performing

*A continuing project since 1978. Have choreographed
a variety of popular songs and performed them in sign
language for the deaf and hearing at public and private
functions, including New Jersey Association for the
Deaf (NJAD) State Conventions, 1978 and 1981, and NJAD
Olympic Benefit Show, 1981.

**Professional
Affiliation**

*American Association on Mental Deficiency
*American Speech-Language-Hearing Association

Resume for a Paraprofessional

Jeffrey Jones
232 Elm Street
Bigtown, Missouri 63187
(314) 671-2452

EMPLOYMENT
OBJECTIVE: A position as a Human Service Technician in a
county agency.

EDUCATION: A.A. in Human Service Studies, Bigtown County
College, 1982.

Bigtown High School, Bigtown, Missouri
Graduated with honors in 1980.

EXPERIENCE: Martha Jonson Nursing Home, Bigtown, Missouri
Part-time employment from 1977 to the present.
I assist the nursing staff as requested and run
a Bingo hour and a hobby workshop one evening
each per week.

U.S. Postal Service, Bigtown, Missouri
Worked as part-time MPLSM Operator summers and
during Christmas seasons. 1979 to the present.

HOBBIES: Basketball, swimming, coin collecting, photography.

RELATED
EXPERIENCE: I am currently enrolled in computer programming
classes at Bigtown Community College. I feel this
will enhance my value to local and county agencies
that may demand versatility in their paraprofessional
staff.

REFERENCES: Supplied upon request.

APPENDIX I

Private Health and Human Service Agencies

Accrediting Council for Services for Mentally Retarded and Other
  Developmental Disabled Persons
875 North Michigan Avenue
Chicago, IL 60611

Acoustical Society of America
335 East 45th Street
New York, NY 10010

Alexander Graham Bell Association for the Deaf, Inc.
3417 Volta Place, NW
Washington, DC 20007

American Academy for Cerebral Palsy
University Hospital School
Iowa City, IA 52240

American Association for Health, Physical Education, and
  Recreation
1201 16th Street, NW
Washington, DC 20036

American Association for Rehabilitation Therapy
P.O. Box 93
North Little Rock, AR 72116

American Association for the Education of Severely and
  Profoundly Handicapped
1600 West Armory Way
Garden View Suite
Seattle, WA 98119

American Association of Psychiatric Clinics for Children
250 West 57th Street
Room 1032 Fish Building
New York, NY 10012

American Association of University Affiliated Programs
1100 17th Street, NW
Washington, DC 20036

American Association of Workers for the Blind, Inc.
1151 K Street, NW
Suite 637
Washington, DC 20005

American Association on Mental Deficiency
5201 Connecticut Avenue, NW
Washington, DC 20015

American Brittle Bone Society
Suite LL3
East Marlton Pike
Cherry Hill, NJ 08034

American Cancer Society
219 East 42nd Street
New York, NY 10017

American Coalition of Citizens with Disabilities, Inc.
1346 Connecticut Avenue, NW
Washington, DC 20036

American Corrective Therapy Association, Inc.
811 St. Margaret's Road
Chillicothe, OH 45601

American Deafness and Rehabilitation Association
814 Thayer Avenue
Silver Spring, MD 20910

American Diabetes Association
18 East 48th Street
New York, NY 10017

American Foundation for the Blind, Inc.
15 West 16th Street
New York, NY 10011

American Occupational Therapy Association, Inc.
251 Park Avenue South
New York, NY 10010

American Orthopsychiatric Association, Inc.
1775 Broadway
New York, NY 10019

American Physical Therapy Association
1156 15th Street, NW
Washington, DC 20005

American Psychological Association
1200 17th Street, NW
Washington, DC 20036

American Public Health Association
1015 18th Street, NW
Washington, DC 20036

American Rehabilitation Counseling Association of the
   American Personnel and Guidance Association
1607 New Hampshire Avenue, NW
Washington, DC 20009

American Speech and Hearing Association
9030 Old Georgetown Road
Washington, DC 20014

Arts and the Handicapped
Box 2040, Grand Central Station
New York, NY 10017

Association for Children with Learning Disabilities
5225 Grace Street
Pittsburgh, PA 15236

Association for Mentally Ill Children
12 West 12th Street
New York, NY 10003

Association for Rehabilitation Facilities
5530 Wisconsin Avenue
Washington, DC 20015

Association for the Aid of Crippled Children
345 East 46th Street
New York, NY 10017

Association for the Education of the Visually Handicapped
919 Walnut Street
Fourth Floor
Philadelphia, PA 19107

Association for the Help of Retarded Children
200 Park Avenue South
New York, NY 10003

Bureau for Education of the Handicapped
400 Sixth Street
Donohoe Building
Washington, DC 20202

Center on Human Policy
Division of Special Education and Rehabilitation
Syracuse University
Syracuse, NY 13210

Child Welfare League of America, Inc.
44 East 23rd Street
New York, NY 10010

Clearinghouse on Programs and Research in Child Abuse and
    Neglect
Herner Company
2100 M Street, NW, Suite 316
Washington, DC 20037

Clearinghouse on the Handicapped
388 D South, Portal Building
Washington, DC 20201

Closer Look
National Information Center for the Handicapped
1201 16th Street, NW
Washington, DC 20036

Convention of American Instructors of the Deaf
5034 Wisconsin Avenue, NW
Washington, DC 20016

Council for Children with Behavioral Disorders
1920 Association Drive
Reston, VA 22091

Council for Exceptional Children
Governmental Relations Unit
1920 Association Drive
Reston, VA 22091

Council of Administrators of Special Education
1920 Association Drive
Reston, VA 22091

Council on Education of the Deaf
5034 Wisconsin Avenue, NW
Washington, DC 20016

Division for Children with Learning Disabilities
1920 Association Drive
Reston, VA 22091

Division for the Blind and Physically Handicapped
Library of Congress
Washington, DC 20542

Division of the Physically Handicapped
1920 Association Drive
Reston, VA 22091

Division on Mental Retardation
1920 Association Drive
Reston, VA 22091

Down's Syndrome Congress
8509 Wagon Wheel Road
Alexandria, VA 22309

Easter Seal Research Foundation
National Easter Seal Society for Crippled Children and Adults
2023 West Ogden Avenue
Chicago, IL 60612

Epilepsy Foundation of America
1828 L Street, NW
Washington, DC 20036

Foundation for Exceptional Children
1920 Association Drive
Reston, VA 22091

Goodwill Industries of America
9200 Wisconsin Avenue
Washington, DC 20014

Institute for the Study of Mental Retardation and
    Related Disabilities
103 South First Street
University of Michigan
Ann Arbor, MI 48108

Joseph P. Kennedy, Jr. Foundation
719 13th Street, NW, Suite 510
Washington, DC 20005

Leukemia Society, Inc.
211 East 43rd Street
New York, NY 10017

Muscular Dystrophy Association of America, Inc.
810 Seventh Avenue
New York, NY 10019

National Association for Mental Health, Inc.
10 Columbus Circle, Suite 1300
New York, NY 10019

National Association for Music Therapy, Inc.
P.O. Box 610
Lawrence, KS 66055

National Association for Retarded Citizens
2709 Avenue East
P.O. Box 6109
Arlington, TX 76010

National Association of Coordinators of State Programs for
    the Mentally Retarded
2001 Jefferson Davis Highway
Arlington, VA 22202

National Association of Private Residential Facilities for
    the Mentally Retarded
6269 Leesburg Pike
Falls Church, VA 22044

National Association of Sheltered Workshops and
    Homebound Programs
1522 K Street, NW
Washington, DC 20005

National Association of Social Workers
2 Park Avenue
New York, NY 10016

National Association of the Deaf
814 Thayer Avenue
Silver Spring, MD 20910

National Association of the Physically Handicapped
76 Elm Street
London, OH 43140

National Center on Educational Media and Materials for
   the Handicapped
Ohio State University
Columbus, OH 43210

National Committee, Arts for the Handicapped
1701 K Street, NW, Suite 804
Washington, DC 20006

National Committee for Multihandicapped Children
239 14th Street
Niagara Falls, NY 14303

National Committee for the Prevention of Child Abuse
111 East Wacker Drive, Suite 510
Chicago, IL 60601

National Easter Seal Society for Crippled Children and Adults
2023 West Ogden Avenue
Chicago, IL 60612

National Education Association
1201 16th Street, NW
Washington, DC 20036

National Federation of the Blind
2652 Shasta Road
Berkeley, CA 94708

National Foundation, March of Dimes
Division of Health Information and School Relations
1275 Mamaroneck Avenue
White Plains, NY 10605

National Information Center for Special Educational Materials
University of Southern California
University Park
Los Angeles, CA 90007

National Instructional Materials Information System
Ohio State University
Columbus, OH 43210

National Kidney Foundation
116 East 27th Street
New York, NY 10016

National Multiple Sclerosis Society
257 Park Avenue South
New York, NY 10010

National Rehabilitation Association
1522 K Street, NW
Washington, DC 20005

National Society for Autistic Children
169 Tampa Avenue
Albany, NY 12208

National Society for Autistic Children
Information and Referral Service
306 31st Street
Huntington, WV 25702

National Spina Bifida Association
3433 South Dearborn Street, Suite 319
Chicago, IL 60604

National Technical Institute for the Deaf
Rochester Institute of Technology
Public Information Office
One Lomb Memorial Drive
Rochester, NY 14623

National Therapeutic Recreation Society
1700 Pennsylvania Avenue, NW
Washington, DC 20006

National Wheelchair Athletic Association
4024 62nd Street
Woodside, NY 11377

Parkinson's Disease Foundation
640 West 168th Street
New York, NY 10032

President's Committee on Employment of the Handicapped
U.S. Department of Labor
Washington, DC 20210

President's Committee on Mental Retardation
Regional Office Building #3
7th and D Streets, SW, Room 2614
Washington, DC 20201

Registry of Interpreters for the Deaf
Box 1339
Washington, DC 20013

Seeing Eye Guide
Morristown, NJ 07960

Spina Bifida Association of America
209 Shiloh Drive
Madison, WI 53705

United Cerebral Palsy Association
66 East 34th Street
New York, NY 10016

United Ostomy Association, Inc.
1111 Wilshire Boulevard
Los Angeles, CA 90017

We Are People First
P.O. Box 5208
Salem, OR 97304

APPENDIX II

State Departments of Special Education

Division of Exceptional Children and Youth
State Department of Education
868 State Office Building
Montgomery, AL 36104
(205) 832-3230

Section on Exceptional Children and Youth
Division of Instructional Services
State Department of Education
Pouch F
Juneau, AK 99801
(907) 465-2970

Division of Special Education
State Department of Education
1535 West Jefferson Street
Phoenix, AZ 85007
(602) 271-3183

Division of Instructional Services
State Department of Education
Arch Ford Education Building
Little Rock, AR 72201
(501) 371-2161

Special Education Support Unit
State Department of Education
721 Capitol Mall
Sacramento, CA 95814
(916) 445-4036

Pupil Services Unit
State Department of Education
State Office Building
201 East Colfax Avenue
Denver, CO 80203
(303) 839-2727

Bureau of Pupil Personnel & Special Educational Services
State Department of Education
P.O. Box 2219
Hartford, CT 06116
(203) 566-4383

State Department of Public Instruction
Townsend Building
Dover, DE 19901
(302) 678-5471

Division of Special Educational Programs
415 12th Street, NW
Washington, DC 20004
(202) 724-4018

Bureau of Education for Exceptional Students
State Department of Education
319 Knott Building
Tallahassee, FL 32304
(904) 488-1570/3205

Division of Early Childhood and Special Education
State Department of Education
State Office Building
Atlanta, GA 30334
(404) 656-2678

Special Needs Branch
State Department of Education
Box 2360
Honolulu, HI 96804
(808) 548-6923

Special Education Division
State Department of Education
Len Jordan Building
Boise, ID 83720
(208) 384-2203

Department of Special Education Services
State Department of Education
100 North First Street
Springfield, IL 62777
(217) 782-6601

Division of Special Education
State Department of Public Instruction
229 State House
Indianapolis, IN 46204
(317) 927-0216

Division of Special Education
State Department of Public Instruction
Grimes State Office Building
Des Moines, IA 50319
(515) 281-3176

Division of Special Education
Department of Education
120 East Tenth Street
Topeka, KS 66612
(913) 296-3866

Bureau of Education for Exceptional Children
State Department of Education
West Frankfort Complex
19th Floor Capital Plaza Tower
Frankfort, KY 40601
(502) 564-4970

Special Education Services
State Department of Education
Capitol Station
P.O. Box 44064
Baton Rouge, LA 70804
(504) 342-3641

Division of Special Education
State Department of Educational & Cultural Services
Augusta, ME 04330
(207) 289-3451

Division of Special Education
State Division of Education
P.O. Box 8717, BWI Airport
Baltimore, MD 21240
(301) 796-8300 ext. 256

Division of Special Education
State Department of Education
31 St. James Avenue
Boston, MA 02116
(617) 727-6217

Special Education Services
State Department of Education
P.O. Box 420
Lansing, MI 48902
(517) 373-1695

Special Education Section
State Department of Education
Capitol Square
550 Cedar Street
St. Paul, MN 55101
(612) 296-4163

Division of Special Education
State Department of Education
P.O. Box 771
Jackson, MS 39205
(601) 354-6950

Division of Special Education
Department of Elementary and Secondary Education
P.O. Box 480
Jefferson City, MO 65101
(314) 751-2965

Division of Special Education
Office of the Superintendent of Public Instruction
State Capitol
Helena, MT 59601
(406) 449-2057

Special Education Section
State Department of Education
223 South Tenth Street
Lincoln, NE 68508
(402) 471-2471

Division of Special Education
State Department of Education
400 West King Street, Capitol Complex
Carson City, NV 89701
(702) 885-5700 ext. 214

Division of Special Education
State Department of Education
105 Loudon Road, Building #3
Concord, NH 03301
(603) 271-3741

Division of Special Education
State Department of Education
225 West State Street
Trenton, NJ 08625
(609) 292-7602

Division of Continuing Education
Bureau of Indian Affairs
P.O. Box 1788
123 Fourth Street, SW
Albuquerque, NM 87103
(505) 766-3351

Division of Special Education
State Department of Education
State Educational Building
300 Don Gaspar Avenue
Santa Fe, NM 87503
(505) 827-2793

Office for the Education of Children with
   Handicapping Conditions
State Department of Education
55 Elk Street
Albany, NY 12234
(518) 474-5548

Division for Exceptional Children
State Department of Public Instruction
Raleigh, NC 27611
(919) 733-3921

Division of Special Education
State Department of Public Instruction
State Capitol
Bismarck, ND 58501
(701) 224-2277

Division of Special Education
State Department of Education
933 High Street
Worthington, OH 43085
(614) 466-2650

Division of Special Education
State Department of Education
2500 North Lincoln Street, Suite 263
Oklahoma City, OK 73160
(405) 521-3351

Division of Special Education
State Department of Education
942 Lancaster Drive, NE
Salem, OR 97310
(503) 378-3598

Bureau of Special and Compensatory Education
State Department of Education
P.O. Box 911
Harrisburg, PA 17126
(717) 783-1264

Special Education Programs for Handicapped Children
Department of Education
Box 759
Hato Rey, PR 00919
(809) 764-1255

Division of Special Education
State Department of Education
235 Promenade Street
Providence, RI 02908
(401) 277-3505

Office of Programs for the Handicapped
State Department of Education
Room 309, Rutledge Building
Columbia, SC 29201
(803) 758-7432

Section for Special Education
Division of Elementary & Secondary Education
New State Office Building
Pierre, SD 57501
(605) 773-3678

Division of Education for the Handicapped
State Department of Education
103 Cordell Hull Building
Nashville, TN 37219
(615) 741-2851

Division of Special Education
Texas Education Agency
201 East 11th Street
Austin, TX 78701
(512) 475-3501/3507

Division of Special Education
Utah State Board of Education
250 East Fifth Street South
Salt Lake City, UT 84111
(801) 533-5982

Special Educational and Pupil Personnel Services
State Department of Education
Montpelier, VT 05602
(802) 828-3141

Division of Special Education
Department of Education
P.O. Box 630, Charlotte Amalie
St. Thomas, VI 00801
(809) 774-0100 ext. 213

Division of Special Education
State Department of Education
322 East Grace Street
Richmond, VA 23219
(804) 786-2673

Special Services Section
State Department of Public Instruction
Old Capitol Building
Olympia, WA 98504
(206) 753-2563

Division of Special Education
Student Support System
State Department of Education
Capitol Complex, Room B-057
Charleston, WV 25305
(304) 266-1649

Division of Handicapped Children
State Department of Public Instruction
126 Langdon Street
Madison, WI 53702
(608) 266-1649

Office of Exceptional Children
State Department of Education
Cheyenne, WY 82002
(307) 777-7416

INDEX